Mātrikā's Muse

A Journey to Awakening Through the Senses

LARA SANDERSON

MĀTRIKĀ'S MUSE
A Journey to Awakening Through the Senses

Copyright © 2025 by Lara Sanderson.
All rights reserved.

This book, or parts thereof, may not be reproduced in any form without prior written permission of the author.

Except for the use in any review, no part of this publication may be reproduced, stored in a retrieval system, or transmitted in any form or by any means, electronic, mechanical, photocopying, recording, scanning, or otherwise, without the prior written permission of the author. Thank you for your support of the author's rights.

Swami Muktananda's essential teaching on page 64, "God Dwells Within You As You" is reprinted from "Essential Siddha Yoga Teachings," https://www.siddhayoga.org/teachings/essential.

Book design by Shannon McCafferty Design

Illustrations in this book combine licensed stock photography and original imagery. Special thanks to Michelle Smith-Lewis for the Tara Devī photograph on pp. 160-162.

Published by Seva Press
To contact the author info@larasanderson.com

First Edition, 2025

Print ISBN: 978-0-578-96533-8
Ebook ISBN: 978-0-578-96534-5
Library of Congress Control Number: 2021915644

The information contained in this book is intended to be educational. It should not replace consultation with licensed healthcare professionals when appropriate.

For my **mom**.
For my **teacher**.
For the **gurus**.
For the **seekers**.

OṀ NAMAḤ ŚIVĀYA

Table of Contents

Introduction — 1

PROLOGUE — 6
[Ashram]

GARDEN — 11
[Shakti] — 13
[Guru] — 25

interlude: *Rejoice!* — 40

KITCHEN — 43
[Nourish] — 45
[Prana] — 55

interlude: *unwanting* — 66

STUDIO — 69
[Breathe] — 71
[Enter] — 86
[Body] — 97

interlude: *Emergence*	107
CREATION	109
[Inspire]	111
[Mātrikā]	122
interlude: *rebirth: a love letter*	134
STORM	137
[Moksha]	139
EPILOGUE	158
What Would I Give You?	
Practices	163
Influential Books and Resources	180
Acknowledgments	182

INTRODUCTION

Once I learned to align myself with my inner truth under the guidance of qualified spiritual teachers, my life began to shift in unimaginable ways, accompanied by blessings beyond my wildest dreams. The process of growth can be uncomfortable, but the transmutation makes it well worthwhile. In appreciation of the changes—readily accessible states of peace, happiness, creative flow, and an effortless sense of connectedness and well-being—I've spent years daydreaming of an adequate way to express my gratitude and reverence for this wholeness restored. This long-awaited project of praise—this book—revealed its form during a confluence of seemingly unrelated events leading up to and into the COVID-19 pandemic.

Ten years prior, I had turned devoutly inward after several events of intense loss. Learning to process my own trauma, to stop moving, and to grieve were not skills that I had acquired growing up. Amidst the stepping-stones of a new and primarily solitary path, I welcomed different kinds of friendships with others who were interested in meditation and yoga. As periods of all-consuming sorrow slowly evaporated, I began to dance again. My years of daily journaling for the purpose of self-observation metamorphosized into packages of poems and essays tinged with a newfound hope.

I also reconnected with another original pastime—gardening. My husband and I became increasingly skillful at—and joyful about—growing our own food (even in the short Seattle growing season!), and we began to celebrate more with others around honest, meaningful life experiences and less around superficial topics we no longer found nourishing. A fresh, if unfamiliar, inner contentment was sprouting—one not connected to any single event, object, experience, or "accomplishment." Instead, this peace had no contingencies! It was bubbling up from an emptiness, from the groundlessness of digested grief.

The same quiet voice that had exacted my decade-long interior journey now began to playfully encourage more outer expression. The earliest and easiest ways were to candidly share musings with my small circle of friends on social media or in simple texts and email exchanges when somebody in pain sought my advice and encouragement. It's a privilege when another human being trusts you with their life questions, hurt, or shame, and I enjoy helping. Supportive words are miniature deeds of gratitude. In these intimate offerings and exchanges within myself and with others, a body of insights was coalescing. Rather than continue to feed the algorithms with my formerly secret experiences, I decided to build them a special container of their own—a blog called *Mātrikā's Muse*. I sought out my spiritual teacher's blessing during a weeklong retreat in August 2019.

Mātṛkā originates from Sanskrit, the mother of all languages and the sacred language of Hinduism. In one form, it means "Divine Mother" and represents the supernatural sounds that correspond to the letters of the Sanskrit alphabet. The Divine Mother possesses the "mystical sonoric power" that gives rise to the Universe through her expression.

To simplify: Words matter. Words create matter. What we speak and write is an expression of our energetic body, and it reverberates from us into the world we actively create.

Introduction

Muse originates from *mousa* in Greek, a language that underpins the rich philosophy of the West. Muse is a personified source of inspiration and an act of being absorbed in thought. In embodied form, it is one of the nine mythological goddesses who preside over and generate insight into the arts and sciences. To muse is to reflect on something thoughtfully.

By conjoining the two words *mātrikā* and *muse,* I intended to capture a felt sense of Source through Eastern and Western influences and study. I am Catholic-educated, having received full scholarships from the Sisters of the Sacred Heart and the Jesuits to attend private schools from sixth grade through college. And I am a yogi by way of chosen discipline and my father, who introduced me to mantra and meditation over thirty years ago. Both spiritual orientations are ripe with the mysticism and devotion that inform this work.

The expressions contained here in this book are but fractional emanations of the field from which they originate—energies taking form as words and images. I hope that they point toward that infinite, creative Source of unlimited energy that remains unseen ... until one sits quietly, tapping into Her realms.

As things tend to go on a spiritual journey, unanticipated events followed the receipt of my teacher's blessing. Another yoga teacher-practitioner, a dear colleague, requested that I submit a chapter on "Kundalini awakening" for her much-needed anthology of women's mystical experiences. Uncertain if I could find an appropriate voice to do service to the project, I sought further counsel on the subject of writing about extraordinary events along one's path. My teacher's response: "Write everything with an intention to help others."

Cloaked in this perfect advice—for everything we do, really —I set about contemplating and brainstorming how to tell a tale of awakening in an authentic way that would take the focus off myself—to remove any sense of "doership" from the narrative. Concurrently, my full-time work on a writing website was met with repeated technical obstacles, a familiar sign that I'm directing energy toward an unsuitable project. The part of that project that was working was the development of an eccentric friendship with a young, feisty woman whom I had hired to edit my blog pieces. As it happened, she had just embarked on her own journey to awakening.

She would often talk a lot, and I would listen. On other occasions, she asked many questions, and I answered them. From these dialogues, the roots of *Mātrikā's Muse* began to take hold and outgrow their tiny format: They grew from blog-post–sized pots to a chapter-sized bed of blooms and eventually into the panoramic landscape the Muse requested. The Muse shape-shifted in multiple ways, dancing into each new form that she wanted to become—replete with snags and solutions, ransoms and releases. I could only pray to keep up and give thanks to the many lessons received along the way. The process, beyond my tenacious drive to show up and work, had little to do with me and everything to do with the creative play of consciousness—and its infinite ability to open new pathways within.

This book is the outer manifestation of this inner journey. When the story refused to take form in an easy essay or a self-contained chapter within another's book, I returned to my teacher with an entire manuscript and asked, "Now what?" I'd never done this! What does one do with an unwieldy, unsought outcome? A seasoned author, my teacher recommended a professional editor from the yogic lineage through which we had all received life-altering grace. As we gradually incorporated input inspired by multiple generations of our female spiritual friends and role models, I began to see how such a story might help to open doors for younger women seeking to experience their innate fullness of being.

As a genre, creative nonfiction could most clearly contain my personal experiences on the spiritual path. I needed a medium that could express the interior world of dedicated spiritual inquiry, as well as the creative ways that intuition and insight are revealed when inner awareness is cultivated through focused discipline. For this reason, *Mātrikā's Muse* is a dialogue between two women at different stages on the path of self-discovery. As it is with the experience of non-duality, neither of them is me, both of them are me, and aspects of each of them are me. We are all the Muse as well as the Mātrikā.

Early in the writing, I debated the need to shape this devotional tribute into a public message. It seemed enough to keep it close. But after long talks with my stepdaughter and hearing what she and her friends are feeling and facing, I became further compelled to write this book out of love for her and her peers at large. In a world misshapen by hateful political rhetoric, I found myself longing to walk in support of the young. I admire how bravely they are searching for and discovering new ways to nurture and express their wisdom voices, knowing that there is much, much more to life than winning at social media and making money. But perhaps the new pathways they desire are not so new. They are likely linked to ancient ways, to the kind of deep inner listening practiced by the mystics, sages, and ancestors. Maybe the young are creating new connections to an ancient living prayer—lineal DNA that is waking up in new bodies ablaze with hope.

If this work's circle of beneficial influence goes further than my initial vision, may its blessings resound. Because in the end, what we do to help eliminate the suffering of others is the most important opportunity before us as human beings. After passionate years of working in politics and a lifetime of seeking to know God, my wish is that everyone discovers the courage to develop the inherent power that resides within themselves. When individuals master peace, so too will the communities of the world.

PROLOGUE
[Ashram]

Eternal Lane is a throwback to a quieter time. Maples, pines, and laurels arch generously over the narrow, worn road hugged by the split-cedar fencing. None of this is imagined as a barrier to others—it is more as a marker that you have arrived somewhere new. It's a place of organic respite, away from a world that is endlessly "world-ing."

I turn off the lane to arrive at the *āśrama*. No, it's not a formal ashram run for a religious community. It's a carefully tended, beloved property created for the upliftment of anyone who visits. Long ago, there were gatherings to raise money for charities and political causes and candidates, but over time those activities faded away. Yoga and safe retreat moved to the fore. The purpose of this spot wasn't always so obvious. It was chiseled from a near-decade of refining its features—all that was needed to support a serious spiritual practice while its caretaker remained a householder.

Protecting the ashram and standing watch where one leaves the lane and enters the grounds is *Gaṇeśa*. His black, dancing eyes and massive trunk draw visitors daily to walk the broken stone path and pay homage to his sculptural presence. It took three and a half years for Ganesha to arrive here

Prologue

from India. Now, after another three and a half years, he has removed many obstacles as well as created some to prevent unfortunate events. There was the time when the newly vacant corner home sold instantly because our charming neighbors made an unconditional offer as soon as they laid eyes on his splendid, auspicious form. Then there was the time when, minutes after Ganesha was installed, huge live rodents ran out from under his base and scared off a would-be intruder.

Today, Ganesha's visitors are two delighted grandchildren of our devout Christian neighbors. When we originally placed him here, I worried that this Eastern deity might offend. But I soon learned that sharing sacred symbols, regardless of tradition, naturally helps us connect and enrich our lived experience. Bundled in sweaters and parkas, the children pull up in a cherry-red plastic wagon, antsy to hop out and skip to the tall rock base of the regal, elephant-headed figure. Their smiling faces, with pink cheeks and heads capped in bright-colored hats, meet him only as high as where his massive foot rests on a pair of large rats nibbling *prasād*—deity-blessed sweets. As their small fingers trace the rats' hand-chiseled outlines, their grandad calls out heartily, "Ganesh!" They squeal back, "Ganesh! It's Ganesh!" The frigid air seems to enliven rather than deter them.

As I'm driving past, I tap my car's brakes, slow to a stop, and roll down my window. "Hello! What a marvelously crisp afternoon—are you enjoying yourselves?"

The children's voices, delightful with laughter, are then soothed as their grandad responds, "They love visiting Ganesha, Lila. It's a highlight of their days visiting here."

I wave bye for now and continue making my way further in over the bumpy cobblestone drive to the refuge of my home. I reflect: "*That* is the highlight of my day—to see treasured devotional art welcoming all who visit."

Reaching the back of the entry drive, I step out of the car to peer over the low brick planter, fence, and olive-covered trellis.

My gaze moves over the old, terraced garden and orchard nestled on the steep hillside that slopes downward to face a canvas of native forest. A hidden stream from within the ravine's sleepy belly, filling to its new seasonal height, is singing. I sing back a favorite *mantra*—a sacred sound of transformation—one universal song to greet another.

A big, deep inhalation of cold air tickles my lungs' alveoli and cilia. This festive aliveness encourages my shoulders to rise up, roll back, and release down. The miracle of breath. Ahhh. It does not matter that the sky's deepening gray is threatening to turn to cloudy charcoal, or that the garden beds are now barren, brown, and perhaps frozen, close to fully asleep and dotted by only a few spare cover crops to provide nutrients to next year's inhabitants.

The Crone's chilly wind bites my cheeks and stings my eyes until they water, but it does not frighten me. Yes, she is dark. Not much lives in her presence—she bestows her rapturous love only on the internally-inclined. Within her startling, withered, obsidian beauty, she holds every ecstatic new beginning. Each new dawn. Every returning spring. Any new idea realized. Appearing deathlike, she is actually the emptiness from which all life arises, including the words appearing on this page. She is the cosmic turning of something to nothing into everything.

When I was a child, I had a recurring dream of an ominous entity trying to break into our family home. I would run back and forth between our front and back doors, desperate to secure the premises. My family was not home to help, and I was terrified. No sooner had I locked one door than the entity would be back at the other, trying to find a new way to break in. Just as I did in that dream, I spent much of my life seeking somewhere safe, a place of complete rest and comfort. Now I know there's no such thing. Yet there is this place, this ashram and the sanctity I discovered here: the place that only exists in the now of my heart. Transformed through the work and love of my spiritual practices, it's a place that attracts new friendships, teachers, and meaningful connections to fellow seekers.

GARDEN

"A few feet down the row,
my young friend digs
quick holes with
her trowel."

[Shakti]

Moist soil trickles through my fingers as I cover the lettuce seeds. They will take root in a carefully tended garden, drink the plentiful Pacific Northwest rain, and feast on lucky days of sun. Among flowers, fruit trees, vines, and vegetables, I experience the sacred teachings. Out here, on my knees, I put my hands in the earth and pray.

A few feet down the row, my young friend digs quick holes with her trowel.

"Athena!" I call. "Remember what I've told you? Your hands need to remember the earth."

She puts the trowel aside and frowns, holding her hands out in front of her as though they don't belong to her, as though they're an ill-fitting pair of gloves.

"I can't. I'm sorry."

"Why can't you?"

"I'm afraid."

"Of what?"

"I don't know, Lila." She examines her palms and knuckles.

"You don't want to get dirty?"

"No. No, I—I don't know what I'm afraid of."

"Are you afraid of feeling the earth?"

"That doesn't make sense." She holds her hands flat, centimeters above the dirt, feeling the heat breathing off it. "Why?"

"Maybe you're afraid of feeling your own power."

"My power?"

"*Kuṇḍalinī-Śakti!* Her power is permeating. She's living through you, and you are so afraid of her."

Unsettled, Athena gazes down at her body, like she might see Shakti blooming out of her.

"I don't think I understand. What is Kunda ... what is she?"

"She's the divine force that resides within everybody and everything. But we've been told it's fantastical, and we're trained to fear her."

"Trained?"

"When you were a little girl, did you play dress-up?"

"Yeah, doesn't everyone? Play war, sing, dance, make up short stories? Inevitably become a college theater kid?"

"That's what I did too! I also wrote poetry. They're all ways we celebrate this divine, creative power within." I reach into the loose soil through the sun-heated top layer and deep into the cool, earthen vessel. Planted up to my wrists, I can feel the tiny vibrations of worms, insects, and taproots. "Shakti is the womb, limbs, and alimental milk of Mother Earth. She's the same cosmic power that creates and maintains everything."

Athena grabs a stick and traces a box around a bright, emerging row of baby romaine. "Everything from this lettuce ... up to the massive redwoods?" She looks to the towering giants off in the distance.

"All of it! When I align with her movement within me, I feel her as this living, breathing, scintillating force. Her power is permeating—inside, outside, omnidirectional. Unfortunately, when I was a young woman, I shut her down in order to fit in. I suppressed her power out of fear—at home, in the classroom, the workplace. Survival required sublimation. Or so I thought."

Athena sits back, eyebrows in thick furrows.

"So, I can't look at her power because I can't look at my own?"

"I'm saying she *is* your power. And when you repress her, you repress yourself. Does that feel true to you?"

"I guess I hadn't really thought of it in those terms before. In my last relationship, my partner broke it off because I was 'too intense.' And my former loser boss said the only reason I got promoted to a job better than his was because my shirts were too tight and showed off my breasts. He *knew* I was smarter than he was. And my mom—she's definitely not comfortable with how outspoken and independent I am."

"It's uncomfortable trying to repress your power to make other people feel good. It's a common struggle for women in these bodies we inhabit. My mom was a feminist in the way she thought and acted, but she wouldn't dare put a voice to it!"

"What do you mean?"

"There wasn't a single problem she couldn't solve with her keen mind, creative hands, and hard work. I once watched her pull over after a car crashed in front of us and drag the driver out through his window and up a hill, so he didn't burn when the car caught on fire. Her library was filled with books on communal living, organic farming, recycling to support the environment, and natural childbirth. Having been born in the 1930s, though, she was not encouraged to stand out, speak up, or take the path of her heart."

"So, what did she do?"

"She became judgmental, critical, and disconnected from herself."

"I am so *not* into hanging around people like that."

"Who is? She'd often talk down about other women to me or make disparaging remarks about my sister's or my body. There was an odd, passive competition with others—instead of supporting them and their accomplishments, she'd compare how she was or could do everything better. Even as a little kid, I knew I didn't want to make people feel worse about themselves in my presence—only better, more uplifted!"

"That's kind of sad, Lila. It's like she abandoned all of her dreams you'd seen living in the book topics lining her library shelves."

"I've often pondered where she learned to repress herself—where I learned to repress myself."

"I'd rather know where I learn to express myself," Athena declares. "I feel like I've spent my life trying to make myself smaller. I'm always smiling when I'm actually mad or sad, like it's not acceptable for me to have feelings because I won't be 'attractive' anymore. My feelings get so sporadic—I can be perfectly happy one day and then some little thing, like spilling coffee, makes me scream at my poor, innocent dog."

"My dad used to call that 'MDA.'"

"The drug?"

"No silly, 'misdirected anger.' It floods out into the surrounding environment, like an oil spill."

"Ahh. And then the ocean and all the birds and sea creatures take the brunt of the toxins, even though they've done nothing."

"Emotions are energy, Athena. Think about it as a simple scientific experiment. Say you're filling up a beaker, and suddenly there's a reaction between the elements. Boom! It begins to overflow. Now imagine you put a cap on the beaker and never let the liquid go anywhere. What do you think that does to our body to hold onto that combustible energy?

"So, I'm like a can of Coke that's been shaken up." She chews her upper lip. "That actually feels surprisingly accurate."

"What do you think would happen if you let your emotions come out instead of repressing them? If you just said to yourself, 'Okay. I'm having some really sad feelings right now?'"

"Isn't that wallowing?"

"It's not about sitting in and prolonging the sadness. You're recognizing and acknowledging, 'I'm going through this crappy experience, but it is not who I am.'"

"I guess it's scary to think of just emoting willy-nilly."

"Willy-nilly. That's a cute description. And it sounds wild! I try not to run around foisting self-indulgent dramas of why I'm 'sad' or 'angry' onto others. Rather, I treat these feelings with care and curiosity."

Athena runs her fingernails over her flexed bicep, studying its form and leaving faint white scratches. "If I feel angry now when I'm this disconnected from my body, how much more overpowering will that anger feel when I'm actually connected?"

"Oh, it's powerful, but I wouldn't say overpowering. In my experience, it's cleaner. Anger is anger, and then it's burnt away. Sorrow is sorrow, and it's felt—it feels like my bodily tissues actually release the sorrow. I can cry. And joy! Joy is ebullient joy, like a five-year-old's! I don't deny any of it anymore. I've learned to work *with* it."

"What if you get super-pissed at someone? Like when my ex used to say, 'You talk too much!' or would tell me the reason I'm angry isn't the real reason I'm angry. How would they know? It pisses me off. Don't you think that's okay sometimes?"

"Yes. Sometimes anger is appropriate, Athena. Entirely appropriate and necessary. Anger is an alarm sounding that a boundary has been trespassed. Now, if the fire of anger goes beyond an ethical parameter, it's skillful to develop an ability to intercede and sit oneself down to process it. I might tell the other person, 'This isn't the best time for discussion.' Then I go lock myself in my room."

"What are you doing when sitting in your room?"

"I'm having the experience of anger. Observing its sensations in my body. Listening to my breath and allowing space for it to slow and regulate. I imagine the heat of anger releasing as gray smoke out of my body and into the Universe to rejoin with the clear, open air and light."

"It's like you're dispersing it to the winds."

"Yes—letting go of that which is not serving my well-being—or other's."

"So, if inside and outside powers are all Kundalini Shakti, does that mean we're all just energy condensed into form? Is that why you take the tightness from being mad and work to open it back up again?"

"I know from working with my most challenging feelings that they all change. Metamorphosize. When they do, my outer world experiences do too. Expansion and contraction—both states inevitably open into the other."

"Even the intense contraction of depression can expand?"

"Can you plant the next one right here?" I look over at the last remaining bed that requires tilling and amending.

Jarred back into our present work, Athena follows my extended finger to the hardened patch of dirt adjacent to her latest planting. Sucking in her upper lip, she bravely attempts to carve out a shallow hole with her fingers, but the ground rebuffs her. It's clay-like, practically solid. Undeterred, she digs around and under the dense soil, deeper, deeper. Finally, the dirt pops free. Setting the hard clump aside, she sprinkles a pinch of seeds into the hole. Then, rather than toss the compact dirt aside, she rubs it between her palms. As her speed and pressure build, the soil loosens and rains down into the hole until the seeds are safely covered.

"Nicely done."

She smiles to herself and plunges both hands back into the earth. "It's really liberating."

I leave her to her discovery and walk to the lowest terrace of Devi Gardens to commune with Goddess Tārā. Carved from stone into one of her many forms, she sits bare-breasted and smiling, immersed in meditation. Jewels and flora adorn her upper arms, neck, and mighty crown. A single lotus climbs her left arm and rests atop her shoulder—fully open.

Garden

Om Tāre Tuttāre Ture Svāhā, I chant internally, kneeling on the ground and resting my forehead on Tara's feet. Her mantra guides me to the universal compassionate, protective, and liberating longing we share for this world. When I close my eyes, I hear her speak:

> *The monks challenged me to abandon my path of seeking enlightenment through my female body. Although I was a princess, they threatened that I must be transformed into a man to reach my goal. I reasoned with them: "There is no man or woman or personhood. Attachments to male and female are meaningless and confusing for people with limited knowledge." I vowed to them that, while many desire enlightenment in a man's body, I will forever strive for the benefit of all sentient beings in a woman's body. This vow requires me to serve others in female form in all my subsequent incarnations...*

As I open my eyes, I reenter this world. Athena has descended the terrace to join me and sits a few feet away.

"Who is she, Lila?"

"Her name is Tara. To Hindus, she is one of the ten wisdom goddesses, a manifested form of Shakti. In Buddhism, Tara symbolizes the fearless and compassionate energy of our mind's true nature and a firm resolve to dispel the suffering and fears of all beings."

Plucking a pile of nasturtium and marigold blossoms along with several ripe strawberries from the nearby planter, prayers and intentions come to mind. The first yellow bloom I imagine as my mom happy in her new lifetime. I wish her happiness and place it on Tara's lap. A red berry is infused with supreme love for my dad and the wish for his continued safety and peace. I leave it in Tara's hands. Next, I think of Athena and my desire for her to become free and fully realized, and I set a bright orange flower onto Tara's knee. One by one, I finish this day's bouquet of offerings and bow my head.

"May I do that too?" Athena whispers beside me.

"Of course."

She picks a saffron-hued marigold and twirls it by its stem, watching it whirl between her fingers.

"What do I pray for?"

"Whatever your heart tells you to. Listen."

Athena pans across our fertile surroundings, scouring the garden and me with her eyes.

"No. Listen *inside*."

She shuts her eyes and her lips move lightly, searching for the words. Then she touches the marigold to her forehead and places it reverently at Tara's feet.

"Thank you. That made me feel sort of tingly all over. In a good way, though!" she hurriedly adds.

"I didn't doubt it."

We get up together and wander away from Tara's statue and across the mossy terrace floor. Simultaneously, we begin to walk the garden levels as a labyrinth, letting our secret longings seed themselves outside. The surrounding air is hushed.

"Lila? I've had this dream—can I tell you?"

"One moment, please." I move to the low stone wall behind me, its hard embrace protecting a fecund bed of red and coral rose bushes. I settle atop it, flat on my back. Sweeping my hand across wide-mouthed blooms that are bent and hovering above my belly, I inhale their perfumed scents as they release into the warm air. Athena sits on the ground just below my shoulder and leans against the crooked stones. "Yes?"

She continues. "In the dream, I'm in a desert, surrounded by thousands of snakes. Shimmering, writhing. Everyone around me is terrified, but I feel exhilarated. I proceed to teach everyone how to handle the snakes so that they aren't afraid anymore. What do you think it means?"

"More importantly, what do *you* think it means, Athena?"

Garden

"I'm not sure. All I know is how calm I felt when I was holding them. Happy."

I pick up a smooth stone. It is warm in my hand, sun-soaked. I place it several inches below my navel where my shirt has come untucked, leaving my skin exposed. "I can see that—a connection with your inner power symbolized externally. The serpents might be various forms of artistic expression you had as a child and young woman." I close my eyes, submerged inside, as words begin to surface and assemble. "The process of making art is like handling a serpent, don't you think? An act of communion with the creative force of the Universe, with Kundalini Shakti ... as artists, it's demanded we dance intimately with the divine through the creative impulse. That we become unafraid. We allow ourselves to be bitten by bliss."

"Drop the mic, Lila."

"Fear blocks life."

She half-laughs, discomfited, then grows serious. "That's one of the most profound things ... that's worth a lifetime of reflection."

"Only one lifetime?" I roll my head toward her and open my eyes, smiling.

"I know, I know—probably many lifetimes."

"Three months before my sister died, I became oddly obsessed with snakes. I began gathering them in an art collection. When I got the phone call saying Micheline's body had been found, I realized I had to shed my skin; I would have to transform if I was to live—to be free."

"Do you think your sister would have been liberated—or at least lived—if she'd taken her artistic gifts more seriously?"

"Hard to say. I sensed she was a very young soul. And I know a lot of artists who haven't taken their gifts seriously, who've misunderstood the nature of their own creativity. Who've been bitten harmfully because they haven't taken to the task of grooming their relationship with the serpent. My former adolescent self included!"

"Well, I'm going to take it as a good omen that I was so damn adept at handling all those snakes."

"I think that's wise. It's a magical vision that's been offered in your dream. Have the courage to realize it."

"You know how you said you 'would have to shed your skin to become free'? I know that feeling. Wanting to come out of my skin. There are times when I look at myself and wonder, *Why? Why am I in this body? Why am I in this form? What am I supposed to do with this?* I mean, I remember this one day when I was feeling so alone in this world and alienated by my own mom; I was driving down this big windy hill near my house and thinking, 'I could just turn my car and go over the cliff and not be here anymore.' Suddenly, there was an immediate inner voice saying, 'Don't do it.' As though God were talking to me but from inside of me. I knew right then that I need to appreciate the blessing of this body. But I'm still trying to figure out how to integrate these experiences. At times, it feels weird to be so condensed. Like my skin's too tight."

"You're understanding that everything is unified, yet you've been fractionalized in this physical body. And you would have continued as energy even if you had shed this body. Once total absorption is experienced, it can feel awkward returning to our embodied states."

"Yup." Athena stares up at the three-dimensional clouds passing overhead.

"*Samāveśa*—the complete merging and entering into the divine state—is freeing. Last summer, my stepdaughter and I were walking our dogs on a sweltering day. We were tired, and the pooches were tired, so we all just plopped down on the side of the road in the shelter of some tall grass. We lost words. We lost time and space. Even our forms disappeared completely for a while. Much later, we turned to each other and asked, 'Did you feel that?' Both of us had fallen into a portal of light—glistening, white light. A portal of Consciousness."

"That's wild. And you didn't feel—I don't know—too limited when you came back to the world?"

"No. It felt soft, like acceptance or receiving an embrace. It's like I realigned with and recalled my already, always whole self. When I am transplanting—digging, sweating, and bearing my body weight onto a shovel to unhinge roots—it feels similar. Turning and smelling the sweet soil composed of decayed food scraps and animal waste from years prior. The complexity of things joining together to sustain life reminds me that limitation and separation are perceptions. Whether expanding into consciousness beyond my body or through my body—I'm awake—aware of being held, being only one part of everything, yet completely unseparated."

"Huh. I guess I do feel that sometimes. When I'm hiking, there are times I'll sort of ... disappear into the forest."

"What happens?"

"I become so in tune with the crinkling leaves and their smell of decomposition and those dumb bugs that fly around your head that I stop existing—or, more that I feel so connected that my body doesn't register as 'mine.' But I never thought of that as something as lofty as samavesha. I mean, I'm not a guru or even a yogi—I'm just wandering in the woods."

I tug playfully at her hair.

"See? You can experience samavesha anywhere: a meditation cushion, absorption in cooking, hiking, or even gardening!"

"So, Kundalini is this process of awakening to life through all of your senses?"

"And whether male or female, we all enter that process of awakening through the female body because we are all born into this world through the mother. We inhabit this earth held within the womb of the Goddess."

"Except my namesake, Lila. She was born from Zeus. She had no mother."

"It was also said that Eve came from Adam's rib!"

Athena grimaces. She kneels into the dirt, collects broken tree branches, and throws them out of the garden one by one, watching as they land in the abundant ravine that encircles the orchard, each earth bone splashing as it strikes the brook below. As the last branch disappears, her face softens and she peers over the edge. "Wow. I think I'm starting to understand some things." She pushes herself away from the wall and faces me and the garden. "When your sister died—was that when your Kundalini awakened?"

"Not all at once, no. And I like to think of it as a 'reawakening,' since I believe it was quite awake when I was born and as a child. But when Micheline died, my heart was splayed open. As Rumi says, 'The wound is the place where the light enters you.'"

[Guru]

I feel an urge to stand and clip a few fading roses. Their loose petals float back onto the earth to provide nitrogen for the bush and its next flowers.

"What was Micheline like?"

"She was a hundred things. But I think her best attribute—what I like most to remember—is her kind and protective nature. She helped anyone and any animal in need with whatever food or money she had. She never minded if they were outcasts. She had a heart for those who suffered."

"She sounds beautiful."

"She was beautiful. Her singing voice was exquisite, as were her aquamarine-blue eyes. She had a talent for floral arranging—she channeled it into her popular business, 'Fleurescents.' On extra-busy weekends, I'd sometimes jump in and help her do a wedding or dinner. I still celebrate these happy memories when I make gorgeous bouquets or perform *pūjā*!"

"There's another word I don't know."

"Puja is similar to how we prayed to Tara. We're making offerings to the divine."

"Lila? Were you and Micheline the closest people in your

family? I cannot fathom my sister dying."

"Well, ..."

"Well, what?"

"Well, I couldn't fathom it either—until I had no choice."

"I can see how much you loved her."

"We were unusually close—up until the last decade of her addiction, at least. The first Christmas without her, I was numb, a sleepwalker. My husband took me on a two-week trip in an attempt to comfort me. One night, I lay in bed drinking too much wine in my attempt to feel something again. I wanted—no, needed—to alter my state. Even that didn't work. I was completely stuck—emotionally paralyzed. All the while, my kind husband was fast asleep beside me, snoring, resting. I envied him. My grief was so weighty that I shut down. I felt like a ghost floating through an outer appearance of the living. I did not know if I could live again."

I look over to see if Athena is okay with this detail. Her eyes are wide and fastened to me, and her face has blanched. I do not want to cause her fright.

"It was hard." I set aside my clippers, inhale, and stretch my arms overhead toward the voluminous clouds. As my breath releases, I tilt my chest heavenward and allow the scenery to ease the heaviness passing over my heart center.

"What did you do?" Athena asks eventually, tentatively. "How did you cope?"

"Eventually I realized that I couldn't live in limbo forever. It was either wake up to something much bigger or die. Then I surrendered to feeling utterly lost. I had to go inside myself to find myself—I had to meditate. Strangely, it was only about five minutes a day for years. But something was happening in those five minutes. Consistently turning inward and observing my breath in all its states, I began to process the trauma. Out of the numbness, I eventually arose, gripping grief and then anger from having someone I loved so dearly ripped away."

"Who told you to meditate, Lila?"

"You know that 'immediate inner voice' that stopped you from harming yourself? That. One morning I woke up abruptly at 3 a.m. and realized that I wasn't the one meditating—I was being meditated. God was meditating on me, and that's why I exist."

"So instead of us praying to God—you're saying that we're God's prayers taking form?"

"I believe that is so. It sounds stark, but I do believe: Death was my first guru."

Athena tugs a young dandelion out of the shadow of the rosebush, its roots startled by the sudden exposure.

"I can't believe you chose to keep meditating, Lila. Who meditates when they're miserable?"

"I didn't choose it; it chose me. Many of my long-held guards were removed. Death pulled the rug out abruptly from under my feet."

"It sounds so painful. Does it have to be so painful?"

"It's rarely a clean process. Our egos cling desperately to their elaborate litanies of narratives. They are not the real you, but it sure feels like they are! Aadya says, 'Awakening comes to your door as a bright light, smiling. Then it blasts through your house and smashes all your furniture, prized belongings, and mirrors.'"

"I don't need it to be pretty and fun, but does it always have to come through a dark night of the soul?"

"Not necessarily. Stages of expansion and contraction are inherent to the journey, though. I've gone through periods where I was absorbed in an indescribable field, *samādhi*—meditative union. Coming to, I thought nothing could ever be wrong in the world again. Even a millisecond of that feels like an eternity. Then eventually another intense contraction occurs—like a door slamming shut. And all the thoughts return. Poof! The ecstatic openness? Seemingly gone. Patience has become my friend. Thank goodness I'm a double Taurus—both rising and sun signs! It keeps me grounded. And I'm tenacious."

"Wait—you believe in horoscopes?"

"I believe anything can be a tool for self-study. Is something wrong with that?"

"Not with that. I'm just thinking of how the hell my fiery, bossy Sagittarius self is supposed to find the patience to practice."

She laughs ruefully. "So, what you're saying is, the pain isn't inherent—it comes from comparing the joy of expansion with the pain of contraction."

"And expectations. Everything changes. It opens and closes. Is born and dies. This is *spanda* ... the creative pulsation of all things, our inhaling and exhaling, coming and going. This is why we observe the breath in meditation. When you watch the breath, there is a watcher. You can investigate what it is that lies between the inhalation and exhalation, in the interstices."

I kneel in the herb garden that nestles against the rosebushes, pick a handful of lavender and lemon verbena, and hand half of it to Athena.

"Here! Rub this between your hands and smell. Isn't it invigorating? It's impossible not to feel fantastic out here."

"You're right. I wish I could take a bath in this." She kneads the purple and green bouquet back and forth in her palms, smelling their elixir. Between deep sniffs, she adds, "The problem is, I don't know how to meditate. Well, I mean, I know how to intellectually. But each time I try, my brain is too loud. My thoughts drown everything else out. I end up feeling furious, worse than I did when I started."

"That's totally normal, 'the chattering mind.' Why do you think you feel furious?"

"Because it's obvious I'm not meditating right."

"It sounds like the problem isn't in how you meditate but in the 'shoulds' you put around meditating. Try dropping

Garden

the story of what you think meditating is supposed to be and maybe ask what it wants to be. Sit quietly. Listen for your breath—in whatever form it takes. And as you settle, ask: 'What does my mind and spirit need right now—this very moment?"

She tries.

"They need ..." Her lips purse as she thinks. "They need quiet. Rest. A break. But see, my mind is so vocal that sitting in silence doesn't work."

"What do you think is underneath those constantly moving thoughts? What precedes them? My teacher once went to her Guru in total frustration and said, 'I'm a failure. I can't stop my own mind.' And he told her, 'Your thoughts are just Shakti, creative life force, energy. View them as such.'"

"So, I have too much life force?" She sticks out her tongue at me.

"Maybe. Or maybe you want to try another form of meditation; you're seeing only one of the multitudes you could try. Meditation is a relationship: it can't be stagnant if we want it to last. There are many ways to approach it and deepen it. Playing with different techniques often helps. Some people are visual meditators, while others use audio cues. Some will picture the thoughts as bubbles rising and popping. I like to go for walks and imagine that, instead of breathing, I'm being breathed. The sensation of my lungs filling, ribs expanding and then relaxing, and oxygen's life-giving force flowing from my exterior to the interior organs and back into the environment ... it's sensual! When I experience that, it feels like falling in love with myself."

"Yesterday," Athena says, "when we replanted the olive tree, I remember it feeling so easy, so right. And I had this moment where I thought for the first time, 'Maybe there's nothing wrong with me. Maybe there's something right with me.'"

"Listen to that immediate inner voice. It rarely leads you

astray. And remember: Stay a little playful!"

I toss my remaining lavender buds in an upward arc and watch them rain down, adorning Athena's curly hair with a deconstructed garland. She smiles and flings her handful of buds back at me.

"Now *playful* I can do."

I twirl in place, take in a big, full breath of clean air and feel my shoulders drop, nestling onto my rib basket. Drinking in the plethora of plants and the symphony of singing birds, I close my eyes and consider my own name, *Līlā*—divine play. The way it describes all of reality and the cosmos, 'me' taking form to experience this interplay between the elements and the Universe again. Her taking form uniquely to experience me.

"Take play and delight," I encourage. "It's important to care for ourselves."

Athena finds a small mason jar and fills it with hose water. She amuses herself collecting herbs, lacy foliage, and an entire rainbow of florets, and composes them into a charming nosegay. "I've heard people say that self-care is a radical act."

"It can feel like that."

"I didn't really understand that before. I'm starting to now. It goes against everything I was taught."

"It can feel revolutionary to say to another, 'You might not accept me, but I am going to ask myself what I need, and I'm going to cultivate it.' When my sister died, I gained a lot of weight. I ate to stay grounded, especially while I could hear my sister communicating to me day and night; the veil between us was so thin. And my yoga practice was next to nothing—I'd lie on the floor, make a shape or two, and call it good. I learned to give myself permission to not get up from the floor until I genuinely felt a desire to move. And I honored that. I let it be okay. Hard to imagine, given my former type-A, push-ahead, over-efforting ways."

"I remember reading, 'There are two wings on the bird of

Garden

realization—one is effort, and one is grace.' Yet we are taught to focus mostly on effort. To push and push and push."

"Sometimes, we push until it breaks."

Together, we drink in the cooling, moist air. Finally, Athena says, "My little voice is so quiet most of the time. Sometimes I'm afraid I'm too far gone, that I'll never be able to find my gut instinct or trust my inner voice again. How do I help it grow?"

"Start slowly. Perhaps like I did. Take five minutes a day—schedule it. Time it. Commit. Sit down alone. Attune to your breath and ask, 'What am I sensing?' Once you find sensation, find a feeling or emotion that arises. Inquire: 'Who is experiencing this feeling?' Teasing these things apart reveals a gap between the knower and the known. There we discover what we are—not some script of who we are or should be."

"That gives me something to actually do—practice—instead of sitting there on the merry-go-round of thinking I shouldn't be thinking."

"We can employ our minds to inquire into their nature. I love meditation because it is a practice. Even when it seems imperfect, it slowly attenuates the mental dialogue and disruptive thoughts."

"You make it sound easy."

"It's a journey we choose. Mine is entirely like and yet different from yours—and there's similarity! It is wonderful to lose the mental lists of things that I once believed to be wrong with me. If that were all this journey's gotten me, that would be significant. With devotion to truth, though, liberation is possible. It's why I continue to meditate and study every day." A warm, sudden gust of wind passes through the clean vegetable rows, spurring me on. "Do you have a guide yet?"

Athena shakes her head. "I want a teacher," she says. "I feel untethered. But it's so hard to know who to trust. It seems like a lot of people pursue yoga for a good body or some cute photos. I mean, 'Happy-hour yoga?' 'Goat yoga?'" She rolls her eyes. "Sorry, I shouldn't get started. But even the teachers who are taking things more seriously—many of them seem like they mainly want power or notoriety. They give a lot of erudite answers. I guess I admire that. Yet, I still feel as though my answers are within me. I'm simply struggling to identify them, to pull them out."

"The guru principle states that 'the guru is you.' The remarkability of nondual tantric practices is that we can do them with ourselves, for ourselves. You can look inside yourself, and through examining your own embodied experience, discover your true Self. Great masters mapped these experiences in detail to help us out, to show us when we're on track and when we're astray."

"I want to feel that level of certainty and acceptance. When I look at my dad, sometimes his devotion to his Guru frightens me."

"You mentioned your dad briefly when we met at the writer's retreat. Your jaw about fell off when you saw I was carrying a copy of *Yogic Disciplines*."

"Well, come on, Lila, really? You have to admit it's not every day you meet someone whose dad is also a devotee of Guru Devi Maa."

"No. No, it's not. Even more peculiar is that I had only just discovered my own dad's copy of that book at his nursing home the day before, dog-eared and fully annotated. My meditation teacher had recommended that I study it long before then. Of course, I'd been avoiding it! Who loves discipline? Going to visit my father and discovering that the very book I was so averse to was standing upright on his bedside table directly facing me—especially when he hasn't been able to read in years—was more than a touch disconcerting. When I packed to go on retreat, I had grabbed it at the last minute."

"Do you know much about their relationship—Guru Devi Maa and your dad?"

"She taught him to meditate. And she gave him a mantra. He followed her instructions devotedly for over thirty years. Every day and every night for half an hour, he sat in lotus posture—*padmāsana*—on the floor of his simple basement apartment to meditate with the mantra. He was so proud when he could finally fold both feet over his thighs, cross-legged! In front of him was a small water fountain, some houseplants, and the Guru's photograph. That's all I know. You seem to know a lot more about your own dad's path."

"Yeah, I guess I do. My dad was your average strong, liberal, East Coast Jew for his whole life—and then, a couple of years before I was born, he found out about Devi Maa and fell completely head over heels. Maybe that's the wrong verbiage, but he's been entirely devoted to her ever since. I recall him telling me that when he first encountered the Guru's gaze, he assumed she was 'in love with him.' But when he leaned in to kiss her, she whispered, "This is different." At that moment, she began to roar with laughter, and he says his 'heart expanded in a way he'd never known possible.' He gave his life to her right then. Now he meditates, studies yogic scriptures—all of it—and a lot. One time, my mother heard my dad saying mantras in his sleep. I think she was jealous." Athena raises her eyebrows.

"Does it make you envious?"

"I don't know. I'm not jealous that he's so devoted. It's just hard that I can't seem to connect with him about it. He has this big picture of Guru Devi Maa in our living room, and I cannot even look at her."

"Why is that? I see an immense blessing in observing an intellectually robust and virile father fervently devoted to a realized female spiritual master."

"I think I'm afraid, Lila. I'm afraid I'll look at her and feel nothing. And I'm equally afraid I'll look at her and see so much power I won't even know what to do with it." She sighs, forcing the air out, nostrils flared. "And when I try to connect with Dad about his spirituality or his guru, we end up talking in circles—or it's more that I argue with him. I don't get it. He's quite patient with me. But I feel like I'm doing something wrong in trying to understand him through this Western, philosophical framework. And I don't know how to get past that."

"I get it, Athena. I'm a Jesuit-educated Catholic."

"No! Really?"

"*Really* really. For a long time, I was convinced the 'guru principle' in itself was flawed. I read books about gurus, trying to prove the believers wrong. I kept up a solitary meditation practice, and the whole time I was thinking the guru thing was a hoax. Then, six years ago, I was sitting in a winter solstice meditation led by my primary teacher. Right in the midst of her guided instructions, a fiery white tiger appeared, surrounded by kaleidoscopic images. Sending a thunderbolt through my chest, he sternly warned, 'I'm her teacher, do not forget that. I am the Guru, and you are mine.' I could not figure it out ... except I knew I must try. When I traveled to meet my teacher in person for the first time and gain insight into that experience, she explained that the tiger I had seen was her guru. She had served him for many years under the name Swami Durgānanda."

"Durgananda ... that sounds familiar. Isn't there the Goddess Durga?"

"Yes. She's the Mother Goddess and a world protector. Her unfathomable strength arises out of her uniquely potent compassion. And ..."

"And what, Lila?"

"She rides on a tiger's back. In an incalculable flash, everything I'd been experiencing, Athena—all the clues from years up to the time of that meditation vision—became evident. The last time I saw my teacher, I expressed my unending gratitude to her: 'You delivered me into the lap of the gurus. I've never felt so safe and protected.' And she confirmed: 'Yes.

You will be safe forever.'"

"Wow. Look." Athena holds up her arm to show the goosebumps.

I laugh and pat her sun-warmed skin. "I know. Is the guru issue what's held you back from the yogic path? Or a lack of mentorship?"

"That's some of it, for sure. Diving into the academics of it and all the fancy terms, or even more so, the intense practices—it feels scary doing it alone. Like I could get it all wrong. But avoiding the spiritual side to do only some of the physical stuff, like taking yoga classes in a fancy studio, feels—I don't know, kinda 'commercial.' This, though ... being here with you ... feels different."

"I am glad you feel safe, Athena. You are."

"So, I really don't have to force myself into a lineage or go after a guru? I can feel the right way in my body and gravitate there?"

"Our bodies are encoded with wisdom. When I recalled my lineage, it physically felt as though my kite finally became anchored. That no matter how far I travel, it will hold me forever. My teacher's guru told her when she was afraid, 'Do not worry ever again; no matter how far you go, I will always come find you.' That story forever makes me cry."

I stop to touch the tears I feel sliding down my inner cheeks, tracing a path to my upper lip. Pooling in the Cupid's bow, my tongue reaches up to greet their warm and salty landing. This taste of now. "The gurus are infinite protection, Athena. They are unshakable support."

"Like the twine that holds up these tomato plants." She tweaks a coiled green fruit hanging from the bamboo frame.

My eyes turn to the curly cucumber tendrils nearby, their perfect spirals guiding them up and up to the trellis top.

"And these!" I point, then throw my arms wide open. "Ta-daa!"

Athena giggles. "You're funny. Everything delights you."

"The world is exceptionally delightful."

"And you don't even seem like you're trying. I don't see you having to focus every second of every day on being present. You know?"

"When Kundalini awakens, her subtle energy demands presence. It becomes nearly impossible to avoid it. She continually uncoils within, whether you pay attention or not."

"Like the vines."

"Exactly."

She wraps her fingers around a loose cucumber vine, watching its pressure flush her skin white.

"I think another big thing that's held me back is the fear of pain and loss. I'm so used to avoiding it. I almost feel guilty when I let myself sit with negative feelings like depression or self-loathing instead of trying to find a way out of them."

"Guilt often comes from feeling like we're not doing something we know we should. Is there something you think you should be doing?"

"Well, yeah. Helping more. Doing more to better things instead of telling everyone else what they should be doing. I complain a lot and focus on what's wrong all the time."

"But Athena, if you are avoiding attending to your own tough feelings with compassion, how will you have compassion for others in need? Or know what needs to be done?"

"Last year, I broke my ankle, and I tried to sit with that awfulness, the intense feeling of fire and self-pity. At a surprise moment, the searing pain just dissolved into energy, tiny particles of vibration. I could imagine them moving beyond my own skin. Then it returned to awfulness."

"Remember that. Keep tending to your pain as something that can be dissolved. Nondualism teachings indicate that in tending to strong sensations—including those we label 'negative'—we access openings to expanded states of consciousness, if we can work with them instead of avoiding them."

"But is the dissolving of pain the same as the 'dissolving'

of self? The samavesha, you called it? Isn't it painful to lose so much of who you are?"

"I wouldn't call it painful because I don't feel I've lost myself. If anything, letting go of and dissolving the pain has uncovered what I truly am. It's quite sublime. What I thought I was fell away. I stopped attaching to pain and the limiting, false ideas of what I *thought* I was or should be."

"A shedding."

"And a revealing. My heart is present to a more genuine love and compassion than I have ever known. There is more peace, more of the time. Sorrow and grief and joy and gratitude coexist. And I don't cling to my thoughts as often. Come!" I wave her forward with my arm. "Let's go see how the fruit trees are doing!"

We stand together, close in height, and walk toward the orchard. As we pass by the apple trees, Athena reaches up to touch each hard yellow fruit. Then she lets each one rest, undisturbed. She moves to pet the textured bark cloaking the central channel of the "Lady Apple" tree, the oldest apple still growing today. Admiring all of the forms manifesting from the One, I place my hands in my pockets and let them melt onto the tops of my thigh muscles. My own strength, my own flesh—skin of this human fruit.

"There have been times when I've committed to meditation for longer," she says.

"For longer periods of regular practice or for more minutes of sitting?'

"Just days in a row. Never more than twenty minutes at a time. I reached a certain point after a few months when I suddenly felt disconnected from everyone around me. Why? I always thought you pursue enlightenment to feel more connected."

"Were you meditating to escape?"

"I don't think so."

"When you venture into stillness, it can feel like you no

longer exist—or that others matter far less. The void state. It's just a phase. When meditation starts to guide you permanently, you'll feel fewer distinctions between the meditative, walking-around, and dream states. They inform one another. Like a tea bag in water—at some point the tea bleeds so much into the water that the differences within yourself (or between you and others) disappear. Don't worry, we have brains and live in bodies. We still have to eat and tend to our duties. Shhh ... listen ..."

We both fall silent, hearing buzzing insects, light footfalls, and shifting branches. A far-off car horn breaks the ambient nature noise.

"See? As long as we're meant to be alive, the phone will ring or we'll need to pay a bill or go to class. Something will require us to emerge again."

"I want to trust the journey." She pats the apple tree's roots. "And, at the same time, the perfectionist voice inside tells me I should already have found the end of the path."

"Enjoy each discovery. That is the path. For me, it's about waking up in this incarnation as a female body and rewriting all the shame and judgment. I used to be so controlling—a horrible, mechanized dictator to myself. Now I feel such gratitude for life, my body. I'm incredulous at this fragile, tough creation that allows me to continue learning ... this 'Lila Suit.'" I hug myself, the trees casting their dappled, undulating shadows on my bare shoulders.

"You know," Athena says, "when I'm in this garden I don't feel trapped in the endless mental dialogue, thinking of everything I don't want to happen. I'm able to immerse myself in the creation of everything I *do* want to happen. The goodness I can create in this lifetime."

She snatches a fallen green apple off the ground and polishes it on her shirt. We step out from under the fruit trees into the sunshine. The garden radiates expansive warmth.

"A lot of people say the world can't possibly be made of

light." Athena lifts the unripe apple up toward the echoing golden glow. "But look at where we are. Kundalini Shakti, she's everywhere."

Rejoice!

all matter
manifests
from One

the infinitely creative
union, p L *a y* s.

from fire,
unending flames
e
m
e
r
g
e
each divine.

oceanic waves,

forgetting ...

awareness veiled,
forgetting ...

its Mother.

releasing
again, and again

Until ...

re-membering

re-awakening

re-calling

                                        fragmentation,

a small part

from something greater.

Source fire—Womb of sea—Sun's ray—Moon's beam—Night sky's celestial stars.

pristine fragments
of the One.

fleeting
telescoping, journeys

                                          reverting

                                              to One.

KITCHEN

∽

"A root requires the sattva
of the cool, clear
water to grow, along
with the rajas of the sun."

∽

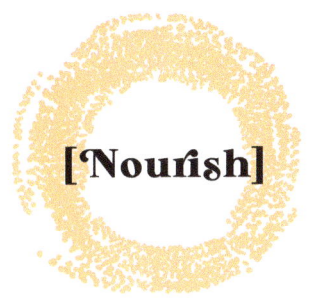

[Nourish]

Rosy late-afternoon light slants sideways through the windows as Athena and I spread our harvest on the countertop. Down the hill, I can still see the proud vegetable rows from which we gathered this soon-to-be feast. I send a silent thank-you to *Devī*, the Goddess, and her gardens, and that which watches over all of life, big and seemingly small.

Athena hums next to me, methodically washing the dirt off the vegetables.

"Did you know trees can talk to one another?" she asks.

"I've heard that."

"They can tell one another if danger is coming, even from miles away. The fungi that live along the roots send the messages. There's even evidence that the roots can 'hear' vibrations and gravitate toward them." She tickles the green onions' white, thready fingers. They quiver. "Sometimes I'm overwhelmed by the liveness of it all."

After the vegetables are washed, I pull out cutting boards and knives.

"What do you want to cook today?"

"I don't care." Her forehead wrinkles. "Whatever."

"Well, is there something you enjoy cooking?"

"Not really."

"Aren't you hungry? I know I am!"

"You can decide, Lila. I'll eat anything." She steps away from the vegetables, her body tense as a fist. But her eyes aren't angry; they're afraid.

Setting down my knife, I offer her an open palm. After a distrusting glance, she places her hand in mine and gasps.

"Your hand is pulsing!"

"Yes. Now, see if you can take a nice, deep breath."

She tries half-heartedly, but she cuts herself off.

"No, I'm fine."

"Really?"

"Really, Lila. I shouldn't slow us down. I should—"

I feel her overactivated nervous system buzzing.

"Athena, all is well. It's okay to wait a bit. Food is an offering. If I'm not feeling harmonious, I don't cook. Food cooked while suffering is not a gift to the person receiving it. Unsettled energy translates into food, even if one's technique is great. Our intentions are potent. So, let's just wait a short while."

"Okay." She reaches for my other hand. I close my eyes and envision the warm light shining in my heart center. Then I begin to direct the light from my heart to hers. She responds with a long sigh. Her tight grasp relaxes, and she aligns her shallow, sharp breathing to the measure of mine. Her inhalations and exhalations steadily become more fluid. Time slows, and we're in sync. When her hands drop, the deep crease that often punctuates her eyebrows is gone.

"You're bumping into a *saṃskāra*. Do you know what that is?"

"Nope."

"Samskaras are like grooves in a vinyl record. From way back in our youth!"

"You know, Lila, those are suddenly 'cool' again."

"Ah, yes, the wheel of life keeps on turning: Everything old is new again." I begin to spin the baby lettuces dry. "Samskaras are impressions stored in our bodies from past experiences. They can make us reactive, less thoughtful, less receptive. Athena?"

"Yeah."

"Do you usually feel this shut-down in the kitchen?"

"Um, yeah. I guess I do. Most people in my generation barely cook."

"Do you know why?"

"Well, I couldn't speak for everyone, but for me, my sister was the chef in the family, and it was 'her thing.' I never wanted to learn. But it also never seems worth it, given how busy my friends and I are with school. I have a hundred other more important things to do in my day."

"Ah, sisters! My sister was 'the singer,' and I was 'the dancer.' Imagine the unexpected delight when I fell in love with chanting—when I discovered I had my own voice!"

"Well, at least we're friendly rivals. Plus, my sister knows I'm the better writer." She crosses the room and gazes over my shoulder.

"Seriously, Athena—if you have to do a hundred important things a day, what could be more important than nourishing yourself?"

"Look, I'll always be able to order food that tastes better than I can make it, so why waste hours of my day on something I don't enjoy and that isn't going to come out well?"

"Sometimes tasting better doesn't mean it's nourishing." I offer her a handful of recently toasted pumpkin seeds sprinkled with pink Himalayan sea salt. "Why do you think your food wouldn't turn out well?"

She crunches vigorously. "Because I always do it wrong."

"I find that when I say 'always' or 'never,' I'm usually not being entirely honest. Things are rarely never or always." I pour us both some water. The sun shining through the glasses paints a rainbow on the opposite wall. "So, why do you believe you cook the wrong way?"

"I'm not just making it up in my head. My ex told me so straight to my face. I chop everything in different sizes, or I get distracted and the food gets overcooked. Oh, and apparently, she thought I added too much salt. It's not fair; I just never learned to do it right—wait." Athena holds up a hand as my lips begin to part. "I know what you're going to say. I haven't learned to do it well—yet."

"Nice catch!" Her smug, knowing look makes me chuckle. "You caught your ego—stirring up trouble! There's no 'right' way to cook, except to do it with love. Perhaps your ex was tied up in their own contracted egoistic drama, judging you. Did you feel it when you were around them? Her?"

"That relationship was with a woman; I'm queer. I care about falling in love with people—not their bodies. Bodies are just the gravy; the goodness on top of it all."

I surmise she's rehearsed this line a bunch. It's cute, and it's a façade. "That's fine. But feeling uptight and criticized is less than ideal, whoever you choose to be in relationship with."

"Yeah. It was so tense in our kitchen. Everything had to be perfect. I was bound to make mistakes."

"Of course. We all make mistakes. And if we pay attention, we learn from them. Have you ever cooked with somebody where it feels differently than that? Maybe fun, or happy?" I wink.

"Not really. I never cooked with my mom—like I said, that's my sister's territory. And my stepmom is an amazing cook, but she doesn't eat the dishes she makes."

"What?"

"She has a ton of dietary restrictions. She'll make food for me and my dad and then ask us to hold a forkful of it to her nose to smell it. That's all she'll let herself do."

"Wow. What a bold statement of self-denial. She supports and sustains everyone around her but not herself."

"I feel guilty eating her food. It's so delicious, and I'd enjoy it much more if I could share in the enjoyment with her."

"Naturally! She sounds *tamasik*."

"What's that mean?"

"It's one of three essential and interrelated energetic properties in the world, the *guṇas*: *tamas*, *rajas*, and *sattva*. In this kitchen, right now, they're all at play! Tamas is the roots, the heaviness, the earth—like our carrots that grow underground in the dark. Behind me, there's the gas stove to cook on flames—rajas. Energy, action, passion. The stove's *rajasik* fire transforms the properties of the cold, hard root veggies." I pick up my glass of water. "And here's sattva! Pure, clean, lucid, and fresh."

"Tamas sounds bad—heavy and dark."

"And why do you think that?"

"You're going to say it's not that simple, that 'everything has its place.'" She widens her eyes and goofily shakes her head side to side.

"When we tune in, we see these energies everywhere and in ourselves. They're morphing and transitioning; assigning good and bad to them isn't useful. Each state simply is—until it isn't. Each characteristic serves its purpose, whether it's inertia, activity, or harmony."

"What's good inertia, Lila?"

I grab a nearby carrot, then my glass. "A root requires the sattva of the cool, clear water to grow, along with the rajas of the sun. The rajasic heat makes them easily digestible through cooking. Then, we eat the tamasic carrots because they're dense with vitamin A, delicious, and grounding for the body."

"I get the heat expanding the carrot's condensed packet of nutrition—unlocking it. But try telling me this stuff when I was five and completely weirded out by my stepmom's heavy behavior with food."

"Fair enough. That would be burdensome to a child. But as an adult, do you see how, if we get stuck in any one energy, it can become habitual?"

"We fall out of balance—into disharmony."

"Yes—and if we stay there, we become entrenched. Your stepmom seems to have consistently shut down. She's cut off, no longer allowing life's creative pulsation to dance within! Healthy food can support and bring balance to all states—if we let it."

"Yeah—if you'll let yourself eat. If you don't eat, you'll die." Digesting our dialogue, Athena folds her arms over her stomach and peers outside at the flourishing green yard. "You seem so happy here—in the kitchen, cooking."

"I am. There's tremendous joy in growing and making food, feeding myself, and feeding loved ones. We should eat as the gods and goddesses we all are." I indicate her untouched glass of water.

"I wish I felt that way about myself."

"Name the exceptional qualities of somebody you love and admire."

"My dad. He's really smart, creative, funny ..."

"Remember: You are all those things too—that's how you're able to identify them! We can tend our special qualities just as we tend the plants you were marveling at today."

For a moment, I feel she may be loosening—but then she turns her back on our harvest and fixes me a hungry look. "Did you ever cook with your mom?"

"Quite often."

"But did you enjoy it?"

"My mom was a great cook, unleashed artistically in the kitchen. She taught me how to make holistic *and* pretty food. Even when she was suffering from cancer, she'd call me and ask with full enthusiasm, 'What have you been cooking lately, Lila?' She'd want to hear all the ingredients and flavors I enjoyed."

"That's so sweet."

"Yes, though during the last time we cooked together in my kitchen, she was alarmingly frail. My mental dialogue kicked up: 'She's so weak, she shouldn't use sharp knives, she'll cut herself,' and so on—then I stopped myself. Coming back to the present moment, I could see that my mother was so happy *right now*. I stayed quiet."

"That must've driven you crazy, though, right? Thinking she could get hurt, having to worry about her instead of enjoying yourself?"

"When I was lost in my mind, sure. But I also truly enjoy supporting others. And when I came back to the truth of the present moment, I was struck by the realization: *Who cares what I think?* We were together, freely moving about space in our tender waltz with few words, slicing veggies, shaking salad dressing, and steaming wild rice. Occasionally Mom would ask, 'What would you like done next, Lila?' It was the last time we cooked as a team. Five months later, she died. Thank God, I allowed her to do what she loved—to be with her daughter, cooking and creating with her hands."

"You're lucky. You were so close to missing that."

"I know. But it was not luck; it was intention."

"But intention without follow-up is meaningless. It can be used as an excuse too."

"My determined focus, Athena, was on envisioning our relationship becoming one of love and understanding. And, yes, to bring that intention to life, I had to learn to drop my critique of all the mistakes I believed she'd made. My action was consciously setting aside useless, righteous quips that continually popped up in our conversations, learning to keep my mouth closed, and observing the power that underlies all things, not only those favorable to me."

"Sometimes people don't act when needed—when it is just to intervene."

"True."

"So how do I identify the difference?"

"Return to locating the cessation between the breaths—the moment between the thoughts, between the inhalation and exhalation. Wisdom arises within silence. It contains an ever-renewing wellspring of truth. That's how loving the Goddess is—we are given infinite chances to reconnect with our innate knowing through awareness. And to discover something new."

"I—I think I know that feeling."

"Yes?"

"This might seem strange ..." she begins, chewing over her words. "Remember when we had lunch at the retreat, and I told you about my bulimia?"

"Of course."

"I'm thinking of a period when it totally overwhelmed my life. I was walking around in this haze all the time. I was constantly hearing white noise. After a meal, I would disappear from my body and tune out, so I could go throw up without shame or guilt. It felt completely mechanical: eat, stand, throw up—not a single thought passing through my head. When I finally got help, my therapist told me to practice finding a pause between eating and vomiting. Thirty seconds, a minute. Even if I couldn't stop myself, I could make myself wait. I could give myself a moment to see the truth of what I was doing to myself. Eventually, that pause lengthened from minutes to hours to years."

"Even the poison can become the nectar, Athena. Or, that by which we fall can become that by which we rise."

"So, even something as ugly and torturous as binging and purging can be a means to spiritual growth?"

"Anything can. Regardless of how it appears on the surface. Are you comfortable sharing why you finally stopped making yourself throw up?"

"The pauses were part of the practice. But the mindset—the desire to stop—came earlier. By the time I found a therapist, I was exhausted. I started throwing up only so someone would realize I was in pain; I wanted someone to notice me. When no one did, I felt this extreme nihilism—this sense that

I was hurting myself for nothing. But by then, I was too far gone to stop without support. In the first session, my therapist told me bluntly that only seventeen percent of people recover from their eating disorders for their whole lives. I decided right then that I would be part of that seventeen percent."

"That single thought and coinciding decision had such influence. *That's* intention with action. You became a witness to yourself. By stepping back, talking back to a statistic, and then practicing as a witness observer for a bit more time between each incident, you healed. Or are you healing yourself?"

Athena nods slowly.

"The yogic sages teach us that if we can maintain our awareness in between thoughts, we see that the automatic or mechanical thought is not what we are. In that moment, we can change the thought as well and redirect our actions. Do something entirely new."

"I guess I'm living proof." A whisper of a smile passes across her face. "It's work, though. Some days I feel so happy to exist in this body, and sometimes food still feels like an enemy I have to fight."

"I understand."

She pauses with a slight frown, perhaps thrown off by my frankness.

"How can you say that? You're—I don't know. You seem so beyond all that."

"A lot of it, sure. But I still need to remind myself sometimes. Maybe that's why you're here."

Athena beams.

"I grew up training to dance ballet professionally. It was my dream. My all-consuming desire! I had so many feelings I could finally express through dancing. As the training intensified, though, it seemed that the more weight I lost, the more acclaim I received from my trainers. I figured that if some attention feels good, more will feel better! I ramped up my physical discipline, restricting myself to under three hundred calories a day. Don't misunderstand—dancing did not cause anorexia."

"What did?"

"A perfect storm of factors: discord breaking out at home and my inability to stop my parents' brutal fighting or my sister running away. I had no idea where she'd live or how she'd survive. It was terrifying for me as a young girl. Starving myself and trying to disappear was more about wanting to escape and control life's uncontrollable nature than it was about being thin."

"You told me you stopped a long time ago, right?"

"I did."

"How?"

"Like you, I was in too much pain for too long. All I was thinking about, all the time, around the clock, was what not to eat. I didn't want to spend the rest of my life in unending obsession. And I began to realize the anorexia was attached to the feeling that I was unlovable. I thought, 'If I can only achieve this goal, then I'll be lovable.' Now I look back and have tremendous compassion. I look at that young, sweet girl and think, 'You always were love, but you couldn't see it.'"

[Praṇa]

She dips her index finger into her water glass and spins it in a circle, watching the miniature waves splash against the sides.

"Do you regret it, Lila? All the pain?"

"I don't regret much anymore. The totality of the experience landed me where I am now. Sure, there are moments I think, 'Wow, I spent a lot of time obsessing about the past or the future, or letting untrue thoughts run roughshod.' What about you?"

"Not really. I still feel really sad sometimes for how much I hurt myself. But since I can't go back and change it, I also focus on how much empathy it taught me—teaches me. Even with my stepmom. When I feel so frustrated with her for denying herself and her body, I remember when I felt that way. I think how much harder it would be to unlock myself from that pattern if I lived in it for fifty or sixty years."

"Surrendering is a lifelong practice. Most things are out of our control. To surrender is to accept that. If I get an urge to impose excessive control on my physical body now, in reaction to the uncertainty, I remind myself: This body is the primary gateway to experiencing God in its magnitude of forms.

And I really don't want to squander the opportunity! What we can do is offer ourselves loving support; we need our bodily vehicles for personal growth. Cooking—and eating—is a lot more enjoyable when I know it helps to sustain and expand my spiritual evolution."

I lean over the countertop and stretch my arms out long, forming an L shape. From my hips all the way up my spine and side and into the recesses of my armpits, I feel a luxurious, opening stretch. As I breathe into the sticky areas for a few rounds, she wanders to the table and scans the vibrant, open kitchen.

"Strangely," Athena murmurs, "you shut down with restriction. I shut down with excess. During my eating-disorder days, I'd overeat constantly. I wasn't even tasting the food—I was completely dissociated. Like I could crush my feelings with the weight of the food in the same way that my mom fills her fridge all the way to the door, so you can't even see what's in there."

"Mine did that too—when she was out of balance. She'd pack the refrigerator with all kinds of stuff she didn't need. Then it would all expire! Even then, she wouldn't throw it out. *Parigraha.*"

"What's paree-gra-ah?"

"It's an opposite of a *yama,* or restraint. In yoga, it's suggested to cultivate nongreed, to observe and question the desire to always have more. Once we're able to take things or leave them behind, the world becomes enjoyable as it is. Happiness is independent of things and status. The constant tossing back and forth between needing and avoiding ceases."

"Or eating and purging."

"Precisely."

"I heard this term once: 'Hungry Ghost.' It feels like the perfect description of who I used to be back then."

"In Tibet, the hungry ghosts are depicted with huge stomachs and tiny little necks. Their bloated desires can never be satisfied, and it literally hurts them to try. When I see them, I think of times I wanted a higher grade, another's acknowledgment, more money, clothes, wine, you name it—the list of useless ways we try to satisfy our hunger can be endless. Desire, in its nature, is unfulfillable wanting."

"I wish my neck wouldn't have allowed the food to go down back then. It would have saved so much effort getting it all back up and out again."

"As grotesque as it seems, Athena, you were trying. Trying to feel—trying to connect—trying to live. I'm glad you're here. I'm glad we're talking about it. Secrets make us sick."

As she traces the sunlit outline of the dining table, Athena lets its sharp edge press into her skin. She eyes the indentation on her finger.

"Is it wrong to still feel angry at my mom? For not teaching me a different relationship with food—with craving? And with myself? I find it so hard to forgive."

"Only you know the answer to that question. Or if it's the most helpful question to ask."

"Would *you* forgive her?"

"That's an even more impossible question. I'll share this instead: Early on in my mom's cancer journey, I had an insight that the tumors forming in her body as hardened, dense places were extreme tamas. I was thinking about it and how her hoarding had overcome her life. Her creative process had come to a complete halt—she stopped painting and writing poetry and music the way she did when I was little. She was uncomfortable when her husband was around—he couldn't or didn't want to see her for all she was. And, maybe out of fear, she didn't allow herself to be seen for everything she was; she shut down her fullness as an artist, poet, and creative wise woman to become merely a wife in exchange for feeling safe. To be with someone who would never hurt her as badly as her abusive stepfather did. It came with an enormous expense. Holding onto all those things pushed her down and, ultimately, it killed her."

"Did you try to tell her, Lila?"

I turn and look out to the striated sunset. A wash of pinkish-purple hues offers the visual fortune of Goddess *Lakṣmī's* abundant, loving comfort. A vase of flowers on the table acquires a warm glow in her generous presence. Sheltered under the flowers and keeping watch sits a carved wooden, wide-eyed owl, a gift from my best friend. As wetness pools in my eyes, I treasure how free and alive I've become over the years. What blessings. All of it. I recall my mom's face and silently tell her, *I miss you, Mama.* I feel Athena's energy pressing in on my still, private moment. If I were alone, I'd meditate. But here, I'm called to serve.

Gently, I push my senses halfway outside again to connect, accepting where I am.

"I told her one time. That's my discipline with anyone I love. Anything beyond that is harping. I visited her in her hospital room and waited until her husband left. I told her what I could see happening in her body and how it connected to her holding onto literally everything while living with somebody perpetually roiling, listening to loud, spiteful, talk radio all day, and dismissing those who disagreed with him. I suggested, 'If you gather the courage to release old, excess stuff, free up new space, and step aside from an inflamed environment, as well as live the way you've dreamed—in a small creative community, with like-minded, thoughtful, artistic people—it might be an invitation to heal.'"

"So, you aren't angry she didn't listen to you?"

"No, Athena. I am no longer mad. She did not choose to act differently, but it was her choice to make. In time, my choice was to develop acceptance that it was her path—and to make decisions about my own. I thank my mom now, a lot. And my grandmother and all the women with whom I share DNA."

"Why?"

"In them, I see myself. I see what happens to me as a

woman if I don't express my creativity, that inbuilt light and artistic nature, my strength, the need to write and sing and dance. If I suppress my nature to make other people comfortable, I'll suffer and die. We will all die, of course, as does everything on Earth. But we don't need to suffer. I thank my mom for teaching me through her suffering how to alleviate my own suffering."

I pause as the melancholic harmonies of the wind chimes filter through the window. When the music settles, I continue, words flowing through like the breeze, the Goddess's breath, my breath, and Athena's.

"I see my path—all of ours—as being to stand and hold a field of light, a vortex that allows our ancestors to speak through us, to forge peace between us. And to respect those who are not able to hold that field; their confusion reveals where we have work to do. Work where the wound is and to stop going around it."

"I admit I do almost everything I can to avoid stuff—situations or people—that have hurt me. I'm really shut down and then pretend to be okay when I'm just not."

"Kundalini Shakti strikes and moves so you can shine, Athena. So that you will be happy, you will attain *ānanda*, the bliss that is your birthright. The Goddess offers us unending examples of how to be and how not to be. We can learn from every one of those examples when we are willing. Everything can be used to release our blockages and support our growth."

We sit silent, placid, listening. The wind chimes start again; this time, their song is simultaneously mournful and joyful. I had hung them outside the window the week my mom died.

Athena gets up from the table and runs her hands over the pile of greens, tomatoes, and carrots we've harvested, now washed and waiting.

"I don't know where to begin," she says slowly. "But I do feel ready to start."

"Good! The fun thing about food in this kitchen is its

intimate connection with the garden. It takes care of me—and those who visit here. The garden tells us what's ready; we don't have to make that decision. I love the enlivening possibility of what can be done only right now with what we have in this present moment. Try it! Select something that speaks to you."

Her hands become rigid again as she hesitantly picks up a few carrots and some ribs of celery. She does not feel them; instead, she moves them mechanically like dead, foreign matter. Her earlier proclamation of sexual certainty superficially guards yet-to-be-discovered experiences of being moved sincerely by life. Touching what's in front of her with sacred wonder will come only with time and trust.

"I'll cut these up. But it won't be a perfect dice," she warns sternly.

"That's just fine. Things are rarely perfect the first few times we do them!" I mince the parsley and oregano into a garnish. A fresh herbal scent fills the room.

"I love these smells," Athena says, waving the scent toward her face. "They wake up my whole body."

"There's the connection. Fresh food feeds our body's *prāṇa*, waking up our life-sustaining force. When I cook, I notice how I'm encouraging pranic flow."

"Did your mother teach you that?" She finishes dicing the carrots and slides the cutting board toward me so I can add them to the pan.

"Probably! I was lucky to be the daughter of a woman ahead of her time. She was raised during the 1940s and subjected to the 1950s. Then, in the 1970s, food became super-processed and prepackaged as more and more women entered the workforce, and they no longer had the time to cook from scratch. Meals became corporate, manufactured."

"What do you mean?"

"Well, long before your generation had so many premade foods, we were introduced to some bold newcomers like Campbell's soups, Marshmallow Creme, and Wonder Bread.

But my mom refused to allow those in our house."

"Really?"

"She'd say, 'No way. That's not good for you—it contains high-fructose corn syrup and hydrogenated oil. It can make you sick.'"

"She knew about high-fructose corn syrup even back then?"

"Told you I was lucky! In hindsight, I think, 'Who was the real yogi?' She truly enjoyed good food—there was plenty of variety in the house—but it was weird hippie food. No Goldfish or Cheez-Its! We had Ak-Mak and Ry-Krisp for crackers, and complex spice blends and rice noodles from fantastic Asian markets. My mom would slice kohlrabi and turnips and feed them to us as chips for snacks. When I was little and realized I hated breakfast, she'd offer to make me anything so I'd have ample brain-fuel for school. I'd tell her, 'I'll eat brown rice and stir-fried zucchini. With soy sauce, of course!'"

"Okay, weirdo." Athena shakes her head.

"I know. But at 7 a.m., my mom had a pot of brown rice and soy sauce ready and would fire up a stir-fry. Or make me homemade raw eggnog in the blender."

"That's kinda cool. Like a real Caesar dressing. Nowadays if you do that, everyone screams, 'Ahhhhh! Don't! You'll get salmonella poisoning!'" She waves her hands frantically.

"My mom perused stores from all different cultures, picking up atypical ingredients the way an artist blends new colors. I learned to value a diversity of vital foods. She knew—whether it manifested in our bodies through nutrition or in our world through agriculture, art, and so on—that diversity is critical for the survival of all beings. That value was reflected in our kitchen."

"I wish I could have seen that or tried to explore it more. Honestly, I feel like a food-processing plant myself sometimes, especially if I'm really busy. I'll make all this food super-fast out of cheap, easy ingredients. The amount of mac and cheese

I ate in college ..."

"And do you enjoy eating that way?"

"Not really. It's like I'm already so amped up from making the food as fast as possible that I can't slow down. I inhale it as fast as I can. Before I've swallowed one bite, I'll shove more food in my mouth. I can finish a whole bowl of something and not remember how it tasted."

"My mom used to say, 'If you relax while you eat, enjoying the quiet or some pleasant company, it helps your digestion.' When she ate, she ate way more slowly than anyone else at the table, chewing each bite a gazillion times. My sister and I teased her, and she'd say it's why she never gained weight! Would you please grab the shiitake mushrooms from the fridge?"

"Part of my problem with cooking," Athena says, pulling out the mushrooms and trimming the stems, "is that I don't even know what to eat. I think, *Oh, I should become a vegetarian, or would I be healthier if I ate less dairy?* And then I get twisted up in this mindset of control. How do I choose the right foods for me without starting to treat myself like a machine again?"

"Observe. Listen. If you crave broccoli, have a bowl of it. Notice how you feel when you're done. Poorly? Energized? Satiated? Hungry? Your body, when you respect it, will report in. Consult your body as you would a dear friend."

"Okay. But what about when I start thinking about controlling things, like no carbs, or this week, I'll only drink smoothies?"

"Just whisper back, 'Shhhhh' and recognize the thoughts happening. Acknowledge the dynamic tension there—between discipline and control. They're easy to confuse. Discipline provides the means to achieve things we want to accomplish on our path. Control is egoistic and can stop us—or tempt us to try to stop others—from doing what we think should or should not be done. Seeking control chokes off life!"

Athena grabs her throat and feigns choking. She rolls her

eyes up and back as we both laugh out loud, catching a big wave of joy. Dropping her hands and catching her breath, she asks, "But seriously, Lila, what's your discipline besides cooking and eating good food?"

"Meditation every day. To go out and tend the garden with awareness. To take in some movement and fresh air." I brush the mushrooms into the sizzling frying pan. "There's a newly baked loaf of bread we could heat in the oven if you like. Why don't you pick out some spices for the stir-fry, too?"

"Sure." She turns on the oven and opens the spice drawer reflexively, as though she's been doing this all her life. "I think I understand what you're saying—that control is repression based in fear, but discipline is a virtue. That said, what does that mean practically? In terms of what I should eat?"

"To some extent, you get to discover that for yourself." I shift the vegetables around in the pan. "I choose what to eat based on what will help me accomplish the things I want to do in this life. Ayurveda, the sister science to yoga, teaches how to care for oneself nutritionally by using various energies. We each have our own *doṣa*, or tendency to particular excesses or imbalances that, left unattended, can impede our well-being. The foods we eat and the activities we partake of during certain times of the day, seasons, and stages of life can reinforce and rebalance us."

"Which dosha is prone to excess anger?"

"*Kapha* is soft, slow, earthy, and patient. *Vāta* is thinner, changeable, more prone to wind-like movement, and creativity. Then *pitta* is outspoken and precise, with strong intellect, but it can easily tip into irritability."

"Then I know what I am. Where I'm unbalanced."

"For some of us, it's super obvious." We share a knowing smile. "I'm fiery. When I am craving excess spicy foods or fried potatoes, I know it's time to cool down with cucumber or melon. And I adore greens! Any kind! I have all my life—because I tend toward pitta, so cleansing, bitter greens feel balancing."

She tosses her trimmings into the compost bucket. "I like that. Choosing foods for balance, not control."

"Approach it as an adventure game: cook and eat to discover which food qualities bring more peace and make you feel good and neutral. And on occasion, if you have too much chocolate or coffee, don't beat yourself up. It can be fun discovering what works."

"Like how we choose when to water the garden and when to let it be." She takes a few measured sips from her glass.

"Athena, here! Take the pan and finish this off for us."

For a moment, it seems she might protest; then she steps into my place behind the frying pan and deftly sprinkles spices and herbs into our dish, mixing them with her spatula. While she does, I put a loaf of multigrain bread into the oven.

"When I cook dinners for my friends, they ask why I make everything so deliberately, so delicious—why it is so pretty, down to my table settings and floral arrangements. I say, 'Because I want you to see yourselves as I see you.'"

"And how do you see them?"

"As deities, worthy of abundant offerings. Various expressions of God, each of them precious and unique in form."

Together, we take out plates and fill them with the stir-fried vegetables and warm bread slathered in ghee. We bring our plates to the table, and she stares at hers, as if unsure where to begin.

"Stick with meditation long enough," I tell her, "and you'll no longer believe that what you eat determines who you are. You discover—or uncover—that you're already whole, already perfect. You've just forgotten the truth. God dwells within you as You, and there's nothing you can do or not do that can change that."

Two tears fall down her freckled cheeks.

"Don't worry," she insists, waving her hand at me. "These are happy tears."

"I'm not worried. Some blockages are clearing."

"That idea really resonates. That I'm not inherently flawed—simply undiscovered."

"You will become much more skillful at saying, 'That's not really me, that's not my big-S Self.' We realize that, after thousands of years, we all come into this body with our own karmic backpack. If we make the honest effort to unpack it, the load does lighten."

"Mmm. Yes." She picks up the fresh loaf of bread and presses it against her lips, breathing in the warmth.

"Do you have a knife?"

"It's okay—tear into it!" I urge.

She does. Then she takes a lingering bite and swallows. "Maybe I've been toting all this shame around for five lifetimes. Maybe someday I'll be able to set it down."

unwanting

i want to reach
through the stacked, empty
calendar boxes
and offer my younger self
sweets
from my open palm

i want to kiss her
with salt on my lips,
remind her that hunger
is not a badge of honor
but a wound,
and its salve

i want to braid my fingers
into her ribs,
bloated with the effort
of contraction,
and teach her to breathe;
to drink air like hot glue
that affixes
her to herself.

i want to unravel
her and follow
her line to me
like hansel and gretel,
but we are the forest
and the witch
and the oven.

instead, i release her

and reach into myself—
into my wide, cosmic space

unboxed and open
still young,

sweet.

STUDIO

> "The ribcage:
> It is a miraculous container sheltering our billowy lungs and pulsating hearts."

[Breathe]

My empty plate catches the last red-orange rays of the day's sunshine, illuminating my contentment. I sit and allow the sensation of fullness to expand within. A sudden rain shower greets the grounds. Quietly, I open my awareness to meet its welcome outpouring. Athena shifts back and forth in her chair, impatiently.

"What do you need?" I ask her.

"Nothing." She seems surprised that I noticed.

"Are you sure? Does your body want to move?"

She frowns, then shuts her eyes as though reaching for something inside herself. When she opens them again, she seems more grounded.

"Yes, I do want to move. That meal left me a bit anxious."

"Here." I slip off my chair and stand. "Let me show you something."

We walk outside, where the rain is already slackening, leaving only the residue scent of creosote and wet timber. Still-gray clouds loom over the garden below, and the rows of emerging sprouts seem cheerfully content with their new, moist reality. Up the hill, we enter the cover of a stand of six enormous evergreens, their tops awash in fog. Beneath them hides an oblong, one-room, cedar-planked structure, inexpertly but proudly built.

"What's this?" she asks, as we tread across a carpet of fallen needles and through a rusty moon gate to the front door.

"A yoga studio. I built it myself, actually."

"When?"

"Oh, a long time ago. Many years before my sister passed. Before I even had a serious practice."

"Sometimes it seems like we become in reverse order." She runs her hand along the smooth door frame, the same color as the graying weather around us. "How did you know to build this before you were even practicing yoga?"

"I can't tell you. I just knew I had to do it. And I knew it had to be placed among these six trees."

"Grandmother trees," she blurts out.

"Why do you call them that?"

"Look up. Doesn't it feel right?"

We both gaze upward at the gnarled branches, the cracked and durable bark. For a moment, time ceases, a familiar phenomenon. I'm uncertain if Athena senses it.

Inside, the studio holds more light than expected at dusk, encouraged by the warm wood flooring and light yellow walls. Along one wall rest yoga mats, blocks, bolsters, and straps. Murals of Tibet, a tapestry of women tending bees together, and pictures of powerful-looking mystics with penetrating eyes watch over the spaciousness of it all. Behind a long, low altar hangs a six-foot-by-four-foot indigenous Australian dot painting.

Athena approaches it, taking in the assemblage of spiritual masters and deities depicted on the canvas, from Gurus and Jesus to Buddha and Mary. There is also *Hevajra* embracing his consort, *Nairātmyā*. All of them are placed within circular cosmic fields of articulated dotting. Interspersed are stars and saints, trees and animals, and clouds and temples, floating telescopically amidst occasional brushstrokes of silver and gold.

"I once read that indigenous Australians painted in these patterns so their spiritual stories would remain hidden when viewed publicly."

"Correct. Certain sacred elements were kept secret from the uninitiated." I join Athena to take in the painting. "To us, it looks like one thing on the surface, but inside, a whole miraculous universe exists."

She scrunches her face and squints. I see she is zeroing in on two small blue-green figures.

"Wh-who are they?" she stutters slightly.

"I believe it is Hevajra embracing Nairatmya. Hold on. I'll look it up." As I retrieve a book that explains Buddhist Tantric deities, I notice her discomfort. She's hushed, and her face remains constricted—she has even turned away. I leave her to her internal dialogue, choosing not to fill the silence. The only thing to break it is the thin crinkle of pages turning as I look for the reference.

"I'm surprised you don't know, Lila."

"Nope. I don't know. It's taken years for me to begin to grasp the breadth of the Hindu Tantric goddesses, so the Tibetan ones will have to await further study! Jamyang, my best spiritual friend and sister, usually helps me with them when I have questions. But since she's not here ..."

"How did you meet her?" Athena's back to studying the picture.

"An uncommon story. I'll definitely share it sometime, but look! I found it ... yes, it's what I thought."

"Are they—having sex?"

"Page 351. Hevajra, the male deity, is shown in sexual union with his consort, Nairatmya. Here—read about the various symbols. It's tough to see all of the details."

I hand her the book.

Athena reads quickly, analytically, voraciously. She shoves the book back to me when she completes the passage.

"Why did you put that painting here, Lila? I mean, it seems to include so many things—representations I haven't heard you talk about."

"Well, a) It's a stunning work of art, and b) I am fascinated by what the artist was trying to convey."

"Which is?"

"It appears that they're making a somewhat serious, as well as humorous, commentary on the major religions. Despite the existence of many forms of elaborate worship, some creation stories were told, quite literally, on the earth—that is, drawn physically in the dirt—as were these, which are outlined in circles and then encircled in dots." With my index finger, I trace some of the patterns hidden in the background. "These originate from initiation rituals—ceremonies that include dance, singing, storytelling, and modifications and painting of the human body. The symbols and patterns vary by tribe and topographic location. Once they were completed, the ritualistically painted designs were smeared to make them unrecognizable. Or they were obliterated."

"All of the small dots remind me of us human beings within the cosmos."

"Mmm, nice. What does that mean to you?"

"That we're each one tiny dot amongst infinite dots, radiating outward. Toward something much bigger, like the sun's rays and the stars." Her voice trails off as she casts her eyes downward.

"That's quite poetic, Athena."

"Thanks."

"If we're within the cosmos, what do you think the cosmos is 'within'?"

"I don't know about the rest of it. Could I have a moment, please?"

"Of course."

She moves hesitantly to the center of the room, eyes darting to each of the four walls and then the ceiling to the floor, up and down. She touches her cheek, shoulder, and then her scalp, stopping abruptly between each point, short of any kind of full stretch. Instead, she shifts her weight uncertainly—from the balls of her feet to her heels and back again.

"What should I do now, Lila?"

"Now? You're welcome to do whatever feels good to do. To tend to, even to caress, the anxiety you spoke about feeling in your body. And I'll do whatever feels good to me in my body."

I sit down and stretch my legs straight out together in front of me, then begin to ease my chest down toward my thighs into *paścimottānāsana*—a forward fold. Gingerly walking my hands toward my feet, I eventually hook my index and middle fingers around my big toes. After several long, silky inhalations and exhalations, the tension at the back of my hamstrings and up my columnar spinal muscles begins to release. My mind calms. Slow, deliberate breathing greets and massages the fibrous tissues between each connecting rib. The ribcage: It is a miraculous container sheltering our billowy lungs and pulsating hearts.

Athena starts to spin in slow circles with her hands half-raised, limp. She looks small and lost. "What's wrong?" I ask.

"Why did you say 'caress'? That sounded weird."

"How so?"

"I don't know—it's too sensual for yoga, somehow."

"Interesting. For me, yoga is a means to touch lovingly into my own body."

She stops spinning and sits down across from me. I sit up.

"I don't— know. I'm not sure what to do. How do I know what feels right?"

"Okay. Let's begin by noticing our breath. A check-in. Start by observing your free, easy breath."

"But it's not free, Lila. Or easy. It feels … stuck."

"Okay. Let's lie down."

"I don't want—I mean I can't lie down right now." Her voice wavers.

In a flash, my mind catches a memory of trauma. Hers or mine ... I check in. In the first moments of knowing my sister was gone forever, I felt as though I could not breathe. Lying down and being still was even scarier—too confrontational. My chest swells with empathy for whatever it is Athena is facing.

"No worries at all. Let's try something else." I retrieve two fluffy bolsters, one for each of us. After handing her one, I show her how to sit on it in *vīrāsana*, or hero(ine)'s pose. We both settle with our knees bent, calves folded underneath our thighs, and hips supported and elevated above our legs. Then I begin anew.

"How does your body feel now? Is this position good?"

"Yes. Much better."

"Would you like some guidance?"

"Yes. Please ..."

"Allow your weight to sink into the cushion. Feel your bones get heavy. Shift slightly side to side, settling in the center. Offer your skin permission to release. Everything sinks down, taking root, receiving the full support of the earth beneath us. If it feels good, allow your eyes to soften and close. If not, maybe soften your gaze. Your spine elongates upward—from this stable, weighted base. The sides of your neck are long, your ears aligned over your shoulders ... skull resting and balancing with ease. Sense your breath ..."

"Lila?"

"Yes?"

"Can I say something?"

"Of course, dear."

"When I keep my eyes slightly open, it feels better—safer."

"Good. So, keep doing that."

I take a moment to pause, letting both of us arrive more fully into our steady seat—*āsana*. She considerately studies how my hands are placed in my lap, on top of my upper thighs, and mirrors them. *Dhyāna mudrā*: my preferred placement for

Studio

meditation. Both palms are face-up, right hand resting on the left hand, the tips of the thumbs touching to form an open circle.

"Continue to notice your breath. Is it shallow? ... quiet? ... slow? Maybe it is quick? ... No need to force or manipulate it. Just observe the breath ... however it is. We'll remain here in observation for another minute or so."

Athena wiggles her bottom, rooting deeper into the bolster's support.

"Now, we'll begin intentional breathing, some *prāṇāyāma*, for relaxation. In this pattern, our exhalation will be double the length of our inhalation. We'll begin with 2 counts in and 4 counts out. Then we'll move to 3 counts in and 6 counts out, and so on. If at any time, it feels forced or too long, let it go. Or stay with the count that feels good. To begin, take a big inhalation in and then let all the air out of your lungs with an audible release."

Athena gasps loudly, like she's gathering breath before diving underwater. She pauses and then forcefully pushes it out with vigor. "*Ph-h-h-h ...*"

"Nice. Now begin to inhale to the count of 2, pause ... and exhale to the count of 4. We'll stay here for a while ... following my count ... now continue on your own.

*
*

*
*
*
*

We're in. As the energy in the room begins to resolve around us, I submit to the vibration of my voice counting steadily and smoothly. I am carried inside the slipstream of the cumulative practices of my teacher and my teachers'

teachers with this eternal means of bridging one back to one's body and beyond one's everlasting home, with the awareness of breath. I externalize momentarily, guiding us into a 3-count inhalation and 6-count exhalation.

Athena inhales for 3 counts and exhales for 6. Her cheeks flush with effort.

"Is this still okay for you?"

Eyes flickering briefly, she states, "Yes, just having some thoughts. Keep going—please."

"It's okay to relocate yourself here, Athena. In the now. Pause and take a moment to look around: What are the surrounding objects? What do you sense? Is there hot or cold air blowing through the vent? What are you hearing? A branch scratching the roof … ?"

As she enacts the suggestion, I do too. Uncertainty lifts. When her gaze resettles, I return to the 3-count inhalation and the 6-count exhalation. My voice trails off once she reconnects within. Knowing not to take it any further this session, I continue to sit and breathe with her at this secure pace. Tension melts from her face.

*
*
*

*
*
*
*
*
*

"As you're ready, ever so gently allow your focus to begin to take in the room. To return here. Maybe move a little."

We both straighten and shake out our legs. Then Athena rolls her head side to side while I curve my spine between flexion and extension.

"This is nice. Thank you."

"You're welcome."

"Your voice is crazy, Lila. I mean, in a good way."

I drift away on a thought, tracing it back to a time when I had no voice. I would stoically push myself and remain active while injured, or say "okay" when coerced to do things against my will. It took decades to develop an ability to speak my inner knowledge and use it to protect myself—despite my work in advocacy and communications. I notice my inhalation. Pause. I release the breath. Pause. In this moment of losing my awareness, awareness returns. Here, with Athena.

"But how does this stuff work in the real world though? Outside of here?"

"You think this isn't real?"

"Of course it is. But you know—when I go back to my place."

"My steadfast go-to is a big 5-count inhalation and 10-count exhalation through pursed lips. I do it two or three times while in traffic or after a charged exchange—it brings me right back to my body. And the present." I demonstrate, feeling the might of my lungs, torso, and lower belly as they fill like a balloon. "When I exhale, I release anything I don't want to carry around."

"Your breath is so big. Fierce." She tries to mirror me but hasn't yet developed the capacity. Her breath gushes out of her, a waterfall. She scowls.

"It comes over time. Not to worry. Now, soften your gaze again. Ask: What does my body want? Any journey to the self begins with asking what is needed. Look to discover what wants to be known."

"But ... what if I don't feel my body?"

"Let's place our hands over our hearts ... apply a touch of pressure. Do you feel something?"

"My heartbeat."

"How does your heartbeat feel?"
"Kind of fast."
"Would it feel good to take a breath in through the region behind the heart, behind the beat, to send some cooling oxygen there?"

She nods and relaxes her eyes. She takes three more rounds of breath. For a moment, a sense of peace returns. On the last breath, she manages to reach a 4-inhalation, 8-exhalation count. Then her jaw tightens. Her eyes open, tears welling up.

"I'm sorry. I ... I guess I haven't asked my body what it needs in a very long time."

"Tears are grace, my teacher says. They mean the heart is opening. When Kundalini rises through the central channel of our subtle body called the *suṣumnā nāḍī*, the seven *cakras*, or energy centers, begin to clear. Long-stored impressions get churned up. It can feel unnerving. But we can completely trust that consciousness is guiding our body in the way it most needs. She moves with perfect wisdom."

Athena wipes at the tears; they glisten on the back of her hand.

"That's a nice thought. Much harder to put into practice."

"Maybe you're trying too hard? It only requires one to show up regularly for oneself, even if nothing seems to be happening. Show up and be tender. Observe without expectations. Occasionally inquire, 'What do I need right now?'" I look away to provide privacy. Out of the corner of my eye, I see her lie flat on the ground and twist her hips from side to side. She repeats the movement, then pauses. Groans.

"I don't know, Lila. I end up feeling so stupid."

"Why? I'm here to listen, if you're willing to explain. 'Stupid' sounds like your head talking—not your heart or your body."

"I see all these people doing yoga or teaching yoga, and they all seem so chill and peaceful when I feel so chaotic. It's like I'll never get there; I can't even understand how they got there."

"You don't feel like you belong?"

"Nope. Or that it will ever work for me. Even when I'm completely alone. No matter how I move, it feels wrong, insufficient, ungraceful. Ridiculous."

"No effort, Athena, regardless of what it seems like, is ever wasted. Past, current, or future—I promise. You'd be surprised at what an anxious perfectionist I used to be."

"Really? Because you seem to just roll with everything. You're even relaxed with traumatic things, like death."

"I am—now. But it doesn't mean I've stopped having feelings about those things."

"Mmm."

"Athena, you do not have to approach everything perfectly for your journey to be worthwhile."

She chews on the thought, jaw working. "Maybe that's what's in the way of my practicing yoga?"

"Or maybe you're afraid to experience life directly, without your conceptual veneer?"

"I do think yoga is supposed to look a certain way."

"There was a time when I stopped myself from everything I wanted to try or learn for fear that I'd do it poorly. But once my sister was gone, I'd make my way here and just lie on the ground. Heavy. Sad. Maybe I'd make a little C-shape bent to my left side, over there ..." I point to a patch on the west side of the room, the memorized grooves and divots that I'd once not known if I could rise from. "Through those windows, I could watch the expanse of gracious ferns unfurling and native maples promising new growth, their generous clusters of crystals blooming from the ground. I could hope ..."

"I can hardly imagine you all bound up like that."

"Yep—I'd lie right there, barely bent to one side with my arm reaching overhead, along my ear. I'd let a tiny little bit of space creep open between my ribs. I'd massage those spots where so much pain was lodged—lungs are the core of grief, after all. I came to accept that my yoga wasn't going to look like anybody else's. Why did I expect my grief to heal when I didn't listen to myself? When I was not taking care of my needs, only everybody else's?"

"Why is it so hard to hear myself?" Athena asks. Her eyes are fixed on the weathered cattle skull hanging at the ceiling juncture between roof and beam—a *memento mori*. "I feel like I've been taught to be deaf to—to be deaf to and to deafen—everything that's happening from here on down." She gestures with a flat palm below her neck, as though cutting off her head.

"Western education trains us that the body and the mind are separate. And now the Westernized view of yoga-as-physical-exercise perpetuates that. But yoga can be a process of integration. For instance, when we slow the physical practices down and coordinate our breath with movement, it soothes the nervous system. The combined practices of movement, breathing, and meditation help restore us from fragmentation. To yoke. To unite. Wouldn't it be great to teach this to children? Let's try something different …"

"Anything. Please."

"Try responding with your intuitive insight and letting go of any judgments that arise. What does your body feel like it wants in this moment?"

"I'm still not sure. What do I feel? I feel too tired to get off the floor."

"Okay. So, stay on the floor."

There's a moment's surprised silence.

Athena says, "I feel … tight. Tight all the way down my left side."

"So why not move your body to the right and elongate the tight space?"

She shifts her hip and sighs. "That feels … good. I can breathe better now."

"How would you like to move next?"

"I think I'm going to stay here a little longer."

"As long as you want. Take as much time as you need."

"Don't I need to do the other side, Lila?"

"Why?"

"I ... I don't know. I was always told to do both sides."

"Ask again: Is this what your body wants to do right now?"

"Nope. Not right now."

"Then stay here as long as you need to. Until it feels right. Check in with your breath. Recognize it. Maybe catch a glimpse of the pause between an inhalation and exhalation. My inhalation tickles my upper lip. My exhalation feels warm. It feels nice."

Outside, the wind whistles by. Nature's breath is emulating our own. The movement makes the trees' leaves shimmy and the windowpanes shiver. At last, Athena sits up.

"How did that feel?" I ask her.

"Like ... surrender."

"Sometimes the only way to get to that place of surrender is to question every single thing you tell yourself and then let it all go. Let it happen another way."

She nods and rolls her head in a slow half-circle—ear to shoulder, chin to chest, and back around—and then shakes out her hands.

"Do I *have* to do yoga?" she says, half-heartedly.

"No. Nobody *has* to do anything. Is that what you really mean?"

"I mean, do I have to do all this? To become awakened."

"No. But I happen to believe it's why we're here. Do you think there's another purpose?"

"Work. Relationships. Accomplishing things."

"Are you feeling a block related to yoga? That could be useful information for me to know."

Her shoulders sink inward, and she nibbles on the corner of her mouth.

"I guess … it's hard for me to want to try yoga because my body feels … uncooperative. Unruly. My whole childhood, I was told how uncoordinated I was. People laughed at the way I moved."

"So many things come easily for you, Athena. When we're praised for all that we do skillfully, there can be a lot more discomfort with things we've yet to experience. Stay curious—like the way you describe being with the environment when you're hiking. Bring a similar openness to the journey inside your body that you do for the outside one."

"I can see what I want to be, ten years down the road."

"And what do you see?"

"I'm comfy in my own skin. I'm in a relationship, a real partnership. A safe one. I can move freely, you know, uninhibited. I have fulfilling work. I express my real opinions."

"I like it!"

"But how will I get there? I won't even take a risk. I'm so afraid of being bad at things—or making mistakes starting out. And I get so frustrated."

"That's an easy but dangerous trap to fall into, especially when we're young. Turning against ourselves with harsh self-criticism. Sometimes it takes only one person to show us another way. Instead of treating your body as something to be materially mastered and sculpted, take an opportunity to play with incorporating our body's guidance."

"You mean instead of looking to be like others?"

"And instead of expecting to look like others! Growing up as a dancer, I was a tyrant to myself, my body. I thought, 'I have this body; it's like a machine. I will force it to do what I expect of it: be rail-thin, have a concave stomach, be excessively flexible.' And so on. But we're not math equations with right and wrong answers. Each body responds to each pose in its own wonder-full, unique ways. There's *Śrī* in that."

"What's shree?"

"Splendor."

"I can believe that in an abstract sense. But when I'm actually in class doing the poses completely wrong, it's embarrassing. And then I feel stupid for being embarrassed."

"What if I told you that you cannot do the poses wrong? They only look different from your expectation of how they should look! Comparison is the thief of joy."

"So maybe I need to let everything be as it is. Stop trying to force it into what I wish it would be."

"Or try not to reject things outright. The minute I do that, I experience whatever I'm rejecting."

"Touché."

"Athena, the Goddess exists in all things—all forms, perfect and imperfect. In each step, whether a baby one or a massive leap. Every single movement of this world is hers. Any experience, despite its surface appearance, will be a portal to our own self-realization. You know what happens when we stop avoiding things? When we stop boxing them into opposites—good and bad, right and wrong? We're finally free to taste the transcendent amidst the mundane."

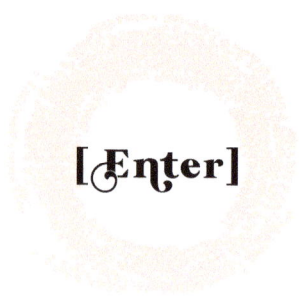

[Enter]

Wind rhythmically washes the studio with easy, repetitive strokes. An inky night peeks in through a skylight sheltering us, our bodies. We drink a cup of chamomile tea made on a small kerosene stove in the corner, served in the two remaining cups from my late mom's Flow Blue china. No words are exchanged. We listen. Rest.

Thump. A grandmother tree drops one of her pinecones onto the metal rooftop. It reopens our exploration of the unknown.

"It's more than the embarrassment of doing the moves wrong, Lila." Athena sets down her cup, stands, and brushes her waist, the curve of her hips. "I think I need to be more honest."

"Honesty is useful."

"When I do yoga in a group, I always end up crying. It's uncontrollable, Lila. Really. It's so strong, like I've never cried before in my life. It's a terrible feeling to be out of control like that in front of strangers."

"Is the pain really from being out of control? Or is it because your heart is opening—expanding—and maybe it doesn't feel safe to open into that in a public yoga class?"

"I can't say exactly that the class doesn't feel safe. It's more that my body doesn't feel safe. When I close my eyes and try to go into my body, I feel like I'm looking into a parking garage at midnight, willing myself to enter."

"Wow, Athena. That sounds intense. And scary. Small wonder you feel like crying."

I get two blankets and spread them on the floor. We sit on them, our backs steadied by walls, facing each other.

"It's inescapable. If I touch myself here—" she prods her upper thigh, "I remember everyone who's ever touched me without my permission. Or I stretch my pelvis, and I remember what it felt like to have someone force their way into my body. All the fury and grief and fear unlock at once ... or I'm terrified it will, so I don't let it." Her hands drop lifelessly to the ground again.

The studio holds us and our silence.

"I'm so sorry you experienced that, Athena."

"I can't even afford to be sorry anymore. My account of sadness is way overdrawn. Truly, I'm exhausted."

"Of course. Fighting to maintain our walls is a full-time job. It's brave in a way, but depleting. Our secrets can make us sick."

"I know my anxiety does that to me."

"So, perhaps the question behind your initial question is really this: How do you begin re-friending your body?"

She sighs, letting the words wash over her. She nods.

"I think you're right. Yeah. I hear from friends and family and therapists that yoga will help, and I want it to. Badly. But after so many years of being disconnected, it all seems so frightening. Nothing feels simple or easy or painless enough to be a baby step. I do a Sun Salute or a Down Dog, but I don't feel it. Not really. I'm only watching myself go through the motions."

"Did you hear what you said? You are 'watching yourself'

Mātrikā's Muse

go through the motions. That statement points at an awareness beyond your body. You're not only your body. Yet your body was violated. Were you raped?"

Startled, she freezes. Softly, I ask, "Is it okay for me to use that word?"

"I've—I've never really wanted to say that. It's so accusatory."

"Athena—uninvited force that violates a boundary is wrong. It is traumatic for the one violated. Humans should not take without asking. Period."

She stares out the window. Her chin rests on her forearms, folded neatly over her bent knees.

"Lila ...?"

"Yes?"

"I've only ever used the word 'assault.'"

"Why?"

"I guess I thought it was more okay to say 'assault.' Less—offensive."

"Lots of people cannot bring themselves to say 'rape.' But when something is violated in a horrendous and coerced manner, whether it's a human body or this planet, it is rape."

"I think—no—I am *feeling* relieved to hear you say that so inviolably. May I come sit next to you?"

"Of course."

She lumbers to my side and plunks down, as though defeated in battle. We peer out into the horizon where descending blue morphs to solid black. Locating oneself in space is no longer available. The void envelopes us, and we sit motionless within the uncompromising, shapeless skyscape.

Tick. Tick. Tick. A small clock reminds me that it's late when I open my eyes. Over an hour has passed. Athena and I lean into each other. My left shoulder abuts her right shoulder.

Studio

The brace of the studio structure strengthens our spines, allowing us to soften elsewhere. Our heads tilt in too, temple to temple. We breathe. She speaks.

"What you were saying before—were you saying that when I felt shame, embarrassment, and a disconnect in classes and saw my body doing moves without really feeling them—that it points to me being something more, something bigger than just my body?"

"Maybe ..." I don't want to tell her anything as she steps bravely forward.

"Hmm. It's weird; I think I am actually feeling better since you were so frank. You didn't tiptoe around the subject of rape and offer some platitude, like 'everything happens for a reason.' And yet what you said—it broke something open. Like my head shifted into my heart. I'm trying to figure it out."

"Athena, really shitty stuff happens in this world. I will never tell you otherwise. And though I can't stop the ground from crumbling under your feet, I can teach you how to become more comfortable when it crumbles. To offer you ways to soothe yourself and find some comfort in your body when things fall apart."

"Thank you. That means something. Have you been through this?"

"Forms of it, I suppose. When I was young, I was quite attractive. People grasped at me when I did not want to be grasped at. Grabbed. They felt desperate to have sexual experiences with me—no, with my body! I was not looking for that. Those people never saw the real me—my spirit—only my body, a source of lust. I stopped enjoying my sensuality and my power."

"What happened?"

"I receded into myself. Became invisible."

"Why, Lila? What did that accomplish?"

"It made some people more comfortable—not having to face their consumptive sexual desires. Desire itself is not wrong. But when desire spills into a compulsion to attain an experience, awareness evaporates."

"So you receded to help others deal with their lack of control? That's jacked."

"That's one way to see it. Another is that my life became simpler and quieter without having to encounter all the passion or envy. In solitude, in my own environment, I could move, dress, and interact in the ways it felt good to me. It was safe. Removing myself from the mainstream world for a long, long time and hiding has been healing."

"Is that why you're here so much now? I mean, you're always here. Especially when I need you."

"I am here because you asked for help. I want to be of help when somebody is earnest enough to request it."

"But why did you let me in—into this hidden, ethereal world of yours?"

"This world is not just mine. It belongs to all living beings. And to our ancestors. Those gone and those to arrive. I created it with my own play, to show my love and unending awe of the gift of life. So that everyone who stepped foot on these grounds and in these gardens can feel the astounding, heart-melting miracle of being alive. Being embodied."

"I hope I can honor that." She traces the soft but pitted pine wall. A few remnant markings of anger remain from bygone years. Dents from prop-supported poses, lashes induced with a strap buckle out of frustration, and scrapes and scratches endured from moving and removing each new piece of tormenting fitness equipment—the elliptical machine, the reformer, the treadmill. None of it is missed now. Neither the machines nor the heavy emotional burdens repetitively beat out in endless circular motion. The wheel of *saṃsāra*, successive states of suffering.

"Honestly, Lila, being around you has shown me that the yogic journey is nothing like what I thought it was. I didn't know it was okay to admit to feeling so much pain. That pain can be welcomed. It's not a weakness."

"Oh my. Heavens no. It takes great strength to speak our truth. One of my repeated prayers is that all of humanity begins to feel safe expressing what's in their heart—Our stories are how we connect as a species—when our hearts fully open, we experience compassion for all living things."

"When you tell your truth and people reject it—a part of you dies. I've had friends leave, partners break things off. I've even had to switch jobs as a result of speaking out."

"Your yogic journey will not be painless, Athena. No one's is. And yet, when something dies, something else wakes up! Something new emerges. I think the worst part of death is the rejection of it. The idea that death should not exist. If we can welcome it, explore what it asks of us, then wisdom—wisdom and inexplicable happiness will surface."

"How do I start to welcome it?"

"Treat death and pain as friends, not as enemies. Imagine them as lonely people with no friends whatsoever. Then, if discomfort arises, go into it, seek its source."

"What's in there?"

"Sometimes there's an accompanying texture or a color. Sometimes physical sensations, like compression or stickiness. Even numbness is a kind of feeling. When I locate the edge of a strong sensation, I deliberately offer my breath into it. I envision the breath dissolving and expanding the edges of the feeling so I can allow it to move through—and not hold onto it."

"I do see a lot of black and dark purple inside when I try to meditate."

"Have you ever asked those colors what they are? Or what they want you to know?"

"That's odd. Colors can talk?"

"If you ask, you might be surprised what you get back! Keep a journal around for these moments. It's informative."

"And what if the pain's too overwhelming initially? Even

for that?"

"Write about it first. Draw a picture. Get it out. On paper, unedited. Let it meet the light of day."

"Maybe that's why I love writing stories."

"Writing is an incredible tool for healing. For speaking our unadulterated truth. And for mapping our trajectory over time. It provides an opportunity to celebrate the entire voyage."

Athena scans the room, taking in all her surroundings.

"I like how it feels in here. It's just the right size. I feel cozy inside this little building, but also when I look outside to the woods. Even while it's hidden from view, I think about it encircling the building. All of it embracing us—our experience."

"Me too. I rediscovered myself here, Athena. Right here, in the safety of this room."

"Hey—"

"Yes?"

"Can we try again, Lila? To find the gap? That space between breaths where you say I can experience what I actually am?"

"I'm happy to, if you like. But remember something—"

"What?"

"Approach every meditation with innocence. Don't expect anything."

"Okay. I will invoke innocence." She smiles.

"Close your eyes."

She glances at me, pupils dilated, fearful again. Then shakes her head minutely. "I—I'm so sorry, Lila."

"Nope! It's my bad. Please don't apologize. I am sorry for not remembering it feels scary for you to close your eyes."

Athena moves her eyes down to the floor, resting her lids at half-mast and gazing steadily about two feet in front of her.

"If it feels okay, begin to notice your breath. If that doesn't feel good, maybe open and close your hands slowly and rhythmically. Or scan your body. Is your knee tight from being bent a while? Is your stomach growling? Does the air touch your cheeks?"

I watch her open and close her hands several times, then rest her palms on top of her thighs. She begins to breathe in and out, pausing for a split second. And then moments later, her furrowed brow relaxes as she draws inward.

"Mmm," she mumbles, pulling herself out of the exercise as though she's uncertain she's allowed to take more than several minutes for relaxation.

"What did you notice?"

"I thought it was going to feel sort of boring doing it a second time, but it made me really aware of myself for a few seconds. Each breath felt so different—each one was new."

"Kind of a miracle, really. That moment. That next new space."

"But isn't focusing on that gap—the one where there's nothing at all—isn't that purposeful split between self and experience another form of dissociating?"

"What a fantastic question. We're not doing anything on purpose; we're noticing that the pause exists, regardless of where our awareness is directed."

"So, what's dissociation?"

"A survival response that protects us from the impact of a traumatic event. But if we remain dissociated over time, feeling that it's unsafe to return to the body, it can wreak physical and mental havoc."

"So, what you're—what we're doing here is creating a safe, new path to reenter."

"Yes. We're accessing our body's innate healing power. When the nervous system calms through yogic practices, the body can process and release old and stored traumas. It restores balance. We are partnering lovingly with our bodies to heal them through the consistent activation of the relaxation response."

"There are times I get injured—like when I tore my tendon last summer—and I'm thrown into these visceral flashbacks. I become so absurdly angry."

"Sure, because new trauma can activate old, unprocessed past trauma. That trigger is a flag that there's still clearing and caring to be done."

She wrings her hands. "When I have the flashbacks, I always end up angry at myself. Not at my rapist."

"My?"

"The—the 'person' ... I feel out of control, like I did after the event. The pain, the injury ... it feels like my body's betraying me."

"If anything, your body is calling you back, Athena. It seems you're not heeding its cry for attention. Has it occurred to you that you like it here because you slow down enough to listen to it? To tap into what you're really feeling versus flitting from one activity to another to avoid the pain? You said: 'I am used to avoiding hard feelings. I always move to find a way out of them.'"

"That's true. A lot of the time, I stand outside of my body. Occasionally, I glance in. I'm more afraid to experience my feelings than I am of the actual event that caused the feelings."

"And what's worse? The violation of your body by someone else or you abandoning your body after the fact? That event is over. But your feelings surrounding the event are not. They want to be recognized, to be welcomed. Recent injuries and new trauma get associated with the old ones, triggering a fight-or-flight response. This happens with not only our personal trauma but also our historical trauma. It is literally inherited from our families' DNA. And it's in our collective DNA as well, in the form of environmental crises, wars, pandemics—and the list goes on and on. It's important not to give up on yourself."

"That makes sense. It also makes a lot more sense why we

need to move our bodies considerately, to release our stored tensions so we can restore balance."

"Athena—"

"Yes."

"I truly hope you do not feel responsible for the rapist's actions. He made a heinous choice."

She opens her arms wide and starts to make big, smooth exaggerated circles, first backward for a few rounds. Then forward for several more, followed by swinging her arms side to side while rotating her torso. She lets out an enormous sigh. "Aaaahhhh ..." Her eyes are steady, no longer scanning the environment.

"Excuse me momentarily—I am not leaving you or your revelation, Athena. I am checking in with myself."

A group of gleaming, silvery angelic forms appear and surround Athena's body, prompting me to close my eyes and study them—to thank them. I wade in further to where thinking diminishes ... into love and surrender, prior to responding. When my eyes open, her protectors are summoned outside, then yonder. I follow them in eyesight only as I stand and approach the window to meet the silhouetted forest, incandescently lit by a tranquil, full, white moon.

"Do you see that tree on the ground? Right out there?" I point to where one of the Grandmothers fell five years ago, her bark decomposing and her trunk stained by winters past.

"I see it."

"Do you see the little pine growing out of it?"

"Yes."

"When you see that great Grandmother being used as a 'nurse log,' do you think of failure or betrayal?"

"Absolutely not."

"So, when we hurt or break down, why do we see it as failure, rather than something that needs our undivided attention? Something worn out, from which something new longs to grow?"

"I don't know. But I guess it's like what Leonard Cohen said: 'There is a crack, a crack in everything. That's how the light gets in.'"

[Body]

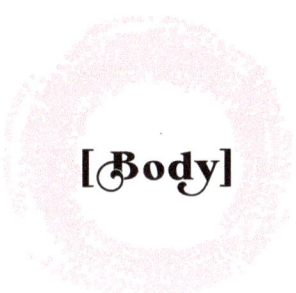

A wispy cloud shuffles across the moon's brilliant face, casting the skinny pine on the nurse log in momentary purple shadow. Athena watches it almost protectively until the cloud has moved on and the tiny tree is once again bathed in moonlight. She whispers, possibly to herself,

"Nature's so ... resilient."

"So are we, Athena."

She looks from the tree up to the moon with concentration. She cocks her head to one side. She covers one eye, then the other. Angles her chin further up. Smiles faintly.

"What are you looking for?"

"The man on the moon. I always used to get excited about finding him as a kid. I just like to remember sometimes that I still can."

Turning away from the window, Athena presses her back against it, stretching her arms out wide to both sides, her palms flat to the cool glass. Her spine straightens, her chest expands, and we breathe together. She exhales, letting everything go. I inhale, taking everything in.

"I'm thinking about what you said," she says without

looking at me. "And about what I've said. Said and done—avoiding my own pain so I don't have to feel it. But, you know, in doing so, it inflicts another kind of violence. Not hearing what wants to be heard from within adds insult to the injury."

"Sometimes we try to solve a problem with a temporary fix that over time becomes a habit. Our Supreme Being becomes shrouded. When we realize this, we can course-correct and make other choices."

"Even when you feel like your body is not part of you anymore?"

"Which part? We have more than one body, you know."

Athena's brows shoot upward and remain high. "We do? That's news to me."

"Our physical body is most evident, like the matter in this forest and the garden. It contains individual elements that we strengthen through our food and yoga poses. It's what most yoga classes focus on in the West. We've become so wrapped up in ... let's just say we allow our identities to be determined by our physicality."

"What about the others?"

"They're more subtle. Our astral body is where our life energy resides. It contains your mind, senses, desires—and the *nāḍīs* and cakras, millions of channels and their hubs through which our vital force circulates. They are Kundalini's superhighways. The astral body is what you're experiencing in your notable lucid dreams."

"How many bodies are there?"

"One more. The causal body. Where joy and bliss reside."

"That sounds like a lot more fun."

"It is also far more subtle. When you're practicing yoga committedly, it becomes more accessible."

"How do you get to it?"

"Through increasing mental quietude and a dismantling of egoistic identification, we begin to feel it. But you don't 'get there.' It pervades all the nested layers and bodies, encompassing all things, and we eventually learn to identify with this consciousness even though we're all the layers of being that it's pervading.

"And what about the bliss?"

"Oh, goodness—*ananda*. It's a homecoming to our true nature. A place where we feel absolute connection and unbound happiness. We lose and remember ourselves, like when you 'fall into' a painting or poem. Or when we look into a beloved's eyes: We merge. Our rapturous absorption in our embodiment as an individual and our absorption in the All—the layers no longer feel separate."

Athena crosses her arms over each other and clasps her elbows. She runs her hands up and down her arms, shoulders to wrists, repetitively. "So, this body is just one part of that experience. But consciousness pervades all of them? Osmosis."

"Yes."

I feel my blood gliding and surging through circulatory channels, reaching far past my once-perceived boundaries of skin, fusing with nature's dynamic web: tree roots to moonbeams, estuaries to lightning flowers, all the way out through the immeasurable cardiovascular network of the cosmos. The rhythm of my heartbeat rises into my head as divine inner instrumentation—I'm being made love to from inside my own body.

"There's something so comforting in that idea." She drops her hands to her sides and looks down at her chest and torso. "That I could recognize, eventually, that whatever was touched, whatever was violated, is not the entirety of me. That those who touched me may think they've gotten something from me, but they didn't get any part of what I really am."

"Your body is a part of you, but it's far from all of you. I know many women—too many women—who've experienced violation as you have. They eventually discover, on the yogic path, that their physical body is not their entirety. Then they're able to set down their stories of shame. It's like taking off a heavy cloak, the lifting of an enormous weight."

"I would do anything to drop this burden."

"I sense that."

"Lila? What did they do to let go of their cloaks?"

"Similar to what we're doing. By continually returning to themselves through asana, meditation, being in nature. There are many choices—options. Our body is our consummate guide, our living, breathing lab. When I map my hardships, they all began with overriding my intuitive wisdom and not honoring my physical body."

"But none of that could stop your sister from overdosing or your mom's cancer."

"No. No, it did not. Nor does it end all hardship. But it did stop me from many unhealthy behaviors that diminished my capacity to face and feel into those events with the fullness of my human capacity."

"I know I ignore my intuitive wisdom." She pauses, caught by the far-off hooting of a barred owl.

My favorite bird arrives. Owl, greeting us. Even this forest royal carries with it the mythologies of dread and death as well as wisdom and protection. "Ha-hoo Hoo Ha-hooo …"

"My gosh, that's magical," Athena coos.

"Ha-hoo Hoo Ha-hooo … Ha-hoo Hoo Ha-hooo," she replies.

Lakshmi's earlier visitation within the mauve sunset concludes with the arrival of her owl, her *vāhana*—vehicle. The Goddess encourages us to seek spiritual wealth over all else. Her owl teaches us to keep our eyes open to the light of wisdom residing within and not to fall into the darkness of ignorance represented by its daytime sleeping. Athena peers at me. The significance of the night bird is reflected in her gaze. I can see her heartbeat fluttering in the base of her throat, fashioning response.

"I want … to become … kinder, Lila."

"Please then, do promise to take dedicated time each day to go inside and know yourself—the self that just spoke. Ask, *What will nourish me? What will help me feel safe? How do I want to move in my body?* Kindness begins with kindness to yourself. Sit quietly. Listen."

"Mmm." She turns and glances out the window again, this time at faraway treetops swaying like dancers in a breeze still too high to reach her. "Let's say I'm able to do that. That I am able to grant myself permission to listen, to cultivate curiosity, and respond gently to myself. How do I take that into a yoga classroom, where it feels like a teacher wants or even expects particular asana sequences to be done in specific ways? Even when it feels wrong for my body?"

"Do not return anywhere your choices are not honored. Do return, again and again, wherever they *are* honored, where you're encouraged to do what feels right. When you find a befitting teacher, a befitting asana, the mantra, you will feel it inside your heart. Honor that. Respect that. Your body is your compass."

"So, what do I do when a male instructor tells me how to do a pose, to line my feet up so close together, but that doesn't feel nice in my body because of these—because of my hips?"

"Stand with your feet apart the width of your hips. Allow space."

"And there are times when they ask you to hold the pose forever, and I get stressed. My breathing gets choppy, and it makes me all anxious inside."

"Release the pose. Sway and gyrate, even bounce a little if it feels good! Allow your breath to regulate itself prior to moving into the next pose. Releasing tension is the goal, not inducing more. A wise teacher, Athena, does not try to control you; they open the primary channel between you and yourself." I jiggle my whole body, shaking and freeing my flesh.

"It feels as though there are so many things—people, rules, images, organizations—trying to control me, my choices, my body."

"Control is an attempt to prevent people from connecting to their power, Athena—to Shakti. When she awakens, it can frighten people. I've experienced this with my own opening. The power is enormous, and when I'm fully connected to it, everyone near me is connected. I hear the entire atmosphere expand."

"What do you hear?"

"Vibration—the air buzzes. Words disband into tones, and forms become frequencies."

"Do you tell anyone?"

"Rarely. I prefer to use Her power to create beauty and space for healing."

"One of my exes loved me only when I was hurting. In the moments when I was able to fully show up, connect, and express myself, he lost interest. Maybe he liked me weak."

"Maybe. Look at any historical dismissal or persecution of people, and you'll see that it's commonly done out of fear of their creative power. This trepidation can deceive people; when that happens, they move to control instead of turning toward one another in support."

"He said he wanted an equal—to not always have to be in charge."

"Which he may have wanted. But sometimes the fullness of Shakti's power, her earth-shattering magnitude, her ability to birth children, and orgasm—her beauty that causes some to fall to their knees with lust—overwhelms people. Instead of surrendering in reverence to that power, one contracts in fear and attempts to suppress it. That's an experience we all have known at one time or another."

"I used to explain to him that feminism isn't the rejection of men. It's the celebration of all genders as mattering equally."

"And an acceptance of all people, as well as an acceptance of all emotional states. We don't need to agree to have that acceptance."

"So then, rejection of either strength or vulnerability—or any quality—is a rejection of one's full self?"

"And one's full experience of consciousness, within which everything exists. Śiva's consort is Shakti, the other half of God. Although it's impossible to apportion the infinite!"

Using her fingers, Athena combs her hair roughly into sections and begins constructing a loose braid. "Could we say 'companion,' Lila? It feels more equal. And it's clear he needs Shakti to create this world."

"Shakti and Shiva—inseparable companions, if you prefer. Without Her, He is not; just as the wind's movement cannot be meted out from the air. They are individual flames undifferentiated from the fire. Differences don't mean disconnection. In fact, it is this connection, this union, that manifests all creation."

Athena stands to her full height. Rooting down through her feet and rising up tall, her chest opens, revealing her full, heavy breasts. She appears primal.

"So, the desire for control comes from fear, and fear comes from an inability to accept that the presence of someone else's power does not reduce your own."

"Furthermore, do not ever allow another's fear to become a reason to repress what you are, Athena. Own your power. Use this power wisely."

She turns to face me. Her eyes remain downcast, searching. Then slowly, they move to meet mine, offering me realization.

"I'd like to believe that everybody, on some level, loves themselves, Lila. Even if they have fallen out of alignment with what that means."

We stand motionless, upright and face to face, resting in the emergent spring of her opening heart-space.

"Pursue your ability to access total alignment with love—the union within. It is the greatest gift."

"And I need this body to discover that ability. My Athena Suit!" Emphatically, she grabs the sides of her bust and playfully presses her flesh into cleavage. She grins, hugging herself and laughing.

"That's what the ancient teachings say. On retreat once, a swami said, 'We're here to grow and we're here to love. We're here to grow our ability to love.' And we cannot do that if we're not embodied, can we? We cannot fathom how many births it took to accumulate the merit of a life in this human form. So now that we have it, what will we use it for?"

Athena walks to the center of the floor and lies on her back, arms by her sides and hips splayed in *śavāsana*. It feels right, and I lie back as well, resting my left hand on my womb and my right hand on my heart, breathing into the points where the center of my beating palm adjoins belly and breastbone. Engulfing white light flows from my heart center into my hands, washing through me, downward into the earth's crystalline, molten core. A rush of heat fountains upward to meet this offering—a mutually reverent recognition of prana—coursing from within this living planet. Through the Earth's mantle, through its oceanic and continental crusts, into the channels of my nervous and venous systems, extending its reach into the studio and into the incalculable space beyond. We yield. We become both heavy and light, submitting to this all-encompassing embrace of bliss.

An undefined exhalation later, Athena languidly rises to a seated position, and I join her. Her eyes, now open, shine like stars.

"I saw it, Lila. I saw inside myself. I saw my pink innards and the blood running through my veins." She lets out a breathless laugh. "I've never experienced that before—the cosmos of my own body. It was only for a second. But it was so, so … beautiful."

"Our body is a portal through which we can experience divinity. It tells us everything we've inherently known forever."

"It's not just a portal," she says. "It's home."

She rises in a slow, pulsating dance, letting her hips and

shoulders sway, vibrating with a vivid fuchsia energy. My body feels content to sit in lotus and watch her, match her expansion. Still swaying, she shuffles to the doors and looks out again at the nurse log, the skinny new pine.

"Isn't it astounding?" she purrs.

"What?"

"The woods, Nature, her life cycles. How she keeps regenerating. There's no end to her. She just keeps unfolding and unfolding and unfolding."

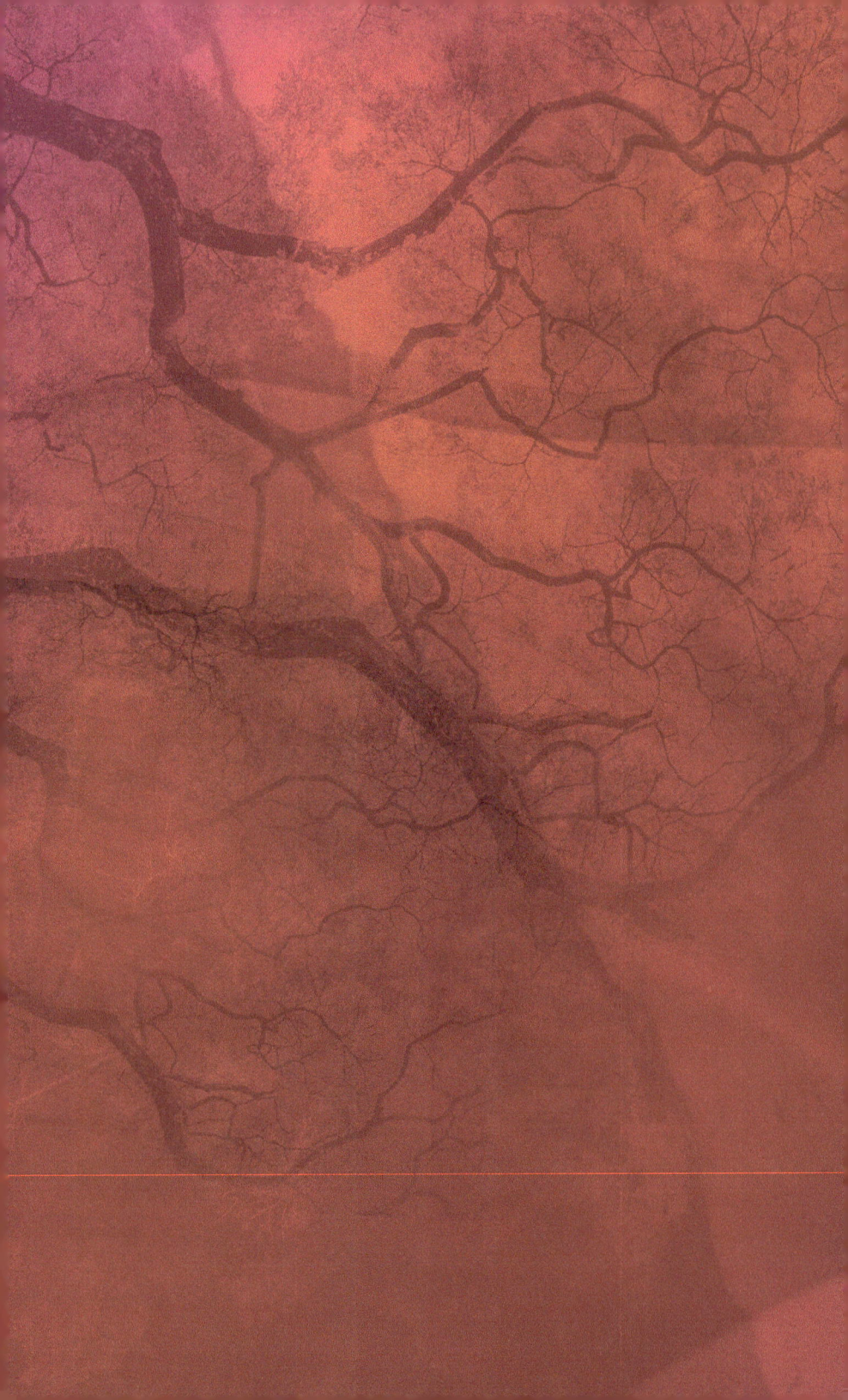

Emergence

Untended. Pushed and molded.
Efforted and sculpted.
Breathing forcefully—in, out, in.

Holding in. Hanging on.
Retaining.
Constantly retraining.

Until

Unexpected. Unpredicted and unprecedented...
Graceful softening...
Breathing ceases—slipping inside...

Releasing outward. Radiating upward.
Surrendering.
Permanently remembering

Awake

This body
Is
Her body
Is
Earth body
Is
Our body
Is
God's body
Is
One
Body
Revealed

What before,
was concealed.

CREATION

"Mātrikā Shakti are
the 'sound packets' that
literally reverberate into matter,
becoming worlds."

[Inspire]

I awake serenely to the earliest morning light, the first birdsong of the day. It's the "Guru Hour"—4:30 a.m. As my fingers trace the curves of my long, sun-kissed limbs, I recite mantras and say a prayer to Her for the grace of how free I feel. My sensuality comforts me in so many ways: the soft, inner pulse of prana tickling my senses throughout the day, whether I'm formally seated for meditation, walking in the forest, dancing, or tending the garden. She is the one who adores me from the inside, who has revealed that I am not an outsider here, not apart from this world's beauty but an undulating aspect of its ever-present light.

After an unknowable period of time, a soft tapping sound at the front door increases in urgency. I roll over, make circles with my hands and feet, and then stretch out for as long as I can for one last lingering moment before reaching for a turquoise robe that is hand-embroidered with birds and butterflies. Its cotton is worn and delicate. The pattern-forming threads have begun to release and fray, blurring their borders and barely grazing my skin.

Making my way to the entry on bare feet, I can already make out Athena's essence from afar. I haven't seen her for a while but am optimistic that she's been finding freedom in her new discoveries.

I pull open the glass door.

"Well, hello!"

"Hi!"

"To what do I owe this pleasant surprise?"

"I have some questions ... I need to go see my mom."

"Need or want?"

She scowls. "It's tough. I thought if you have some time, we could talk? Maybe?"

"I still need to meditate and study this morning. Why don't you come back at around eleven, and we can visit then?"

Her face falls, but she holds herself open.

"Of course." She starts to leave but pauses with a shy glance. "By the way, you look beautiful. I can't believe you're fifty."

"Thank you, Athena. That's a lovely compliment."

"See you later."

"And remember," I call after her, "we can only see in others what we are present to in ourselves."

The earliest flickers of sunshine follow her retreat. I catch a flash of her smile.

༄

"Did you enjoy your study?" she asks.

"Very much. There's so much to learn and appreciate! Where do you want to sit?"

Athena scans the backyard and chooses a smooth patch of grass spreading among the roots of an enormous ponderosa pine. The tree's branches are unusual, forming a massive trident that points skyward. Before she settles in, she presses her nose against the bark and inhales deeply.

"Ahhh."

"What do you smell?"

Creation

"Vanilla. Vanilla and cinnamon."

"Cream and spice. Now you know where I get inspiration for creating in the kitchen."

"What do you do?"

"Follow the qualities of an herb or flower or scent of the earth."

"I get that, but what do you do next?"

"I think about what wants to be created with it. What it is asking to become. Sometimes it's a salad dressing. Other times, it's a marinade or a drink. It's also nice to boil tree branches on the stove to release their aromas into the room."

Sitting cross-legged, her back against the trunk, Athena fiddles with her fingers, twiddling her thumbs around and around each other. She stops as soon as she notices me observing.

"Athena, are you upset that I asked you to return later?"

"No."

"Okay. But your muscles seem guarded, your shoulders high. Are you tense about something?"

"I'm upset at myself."

"Why?"

"Oh, I don't know. I'm sorry."

"Why are you sorry?"

She flinches, and I add, "It might make sense to ask yourself why you're sorry, rather than rush to apologize."

"I feel like I'm ruining your morning, coming in like this, experiencing all this wrong, agitated energy."

"There's no such thing as wrong energy. Some energies are simply more pleasant, more expansive."

"I started thinking—no, wait ..." She closes her eyes and takes a deep breath, releases it slowly, and repeats. Her shoulders drop. "I started worrying that you didn't want me to visit."

"Are you apologizing for asking for something you need?" I smile gently, but she can't look at me. "I used to constantly say 'I'm sorry' when I was young. But there's no need when you've done nothing wrong. At those times, stop apologizing. Don't deny yourself permission to exist as you are. So ... what is it, dear? What are you feeling?"

"I'm—contracting again. And it's uncomfortable. I don't like it. Yesterday, I felt like I was able to give myself permission to open up, expand, express."

"What changed?"

"Today, I got nervous about going home to see my mom. And, poof. Gone. When I first came by, it wasn't so bad, but when you sent me off, I couldn't stop thinking and thinking and thinking about it. About how constricted my mom is, and how I'm afraid that I'll go to visit her and become constricted too, and now—"

"Now you're really feeling constricted, worrying about it?" With intention, I direct my breath down into the well of my belly, a lower source center. Earth energy greets me, entering through my perineum and flowing upward along my spine. Grounded and relaxed, there's spaciousness to hold Athena's full experience.

"Exactly, Lila. Whenever I begin to talk to myself in my head about stuff, over and over and over, my body contracts."

She digs around in the pocket of her skirt, as though just remembering something, and pulls out a crumpled sheet of paper. "I wrote this after I went back home this morning. When we did yoga, you said writing could help release the dark feelings from my body."

"Or bring light to them. Did it help?"

"I thought so at first, since the words flew electrically off my pen. But part of me thinks the writing may have made things worse." She proffers it a few inches toward me, then pulls it back again and holds it close.

"Would you like me to read it?" I open my hand.

Athena tosses the paper to me as if to rid herself of it. Unfolding it, I find a short poem, scrawled in messy cursive.

How to Live Forever

Count the minutes like calories
Feel each one flay away your youth

Trace the deepening lines
Of each irrevocable wrinkle

Save small hanks of your hair
Before it grows gray and limp, like a severed hand

Memorize the thinness of your child's fingers
That will never again be quite so small

Fill shallow boxes with old socks, potpourri,
Strips of pillowcase, tobacco, peppermint

Press your lips against stone
To remember what it meant to yield.

I read it twice, feeling into the words for their invisible, vibrational encryption. When I look up, she is staring at me hungrily. Immediately, she tears her attention away again.

"It's nothing. We don't have to waste time discussing it."

"Athena, we've done this dance before. A lot. Would you or would you not like to work through this?"

"Yes, I would."

"Beyond trying to process some shadowy feelings, I'd love to hear what made you write these words."

"I'm not sure."

"If you look closely at the poem ..." I hand it back to her and rephrase the question. "Why did you select these specific words?"

"Seriously, Lila. I wasn't thinking—at all. I was doing. Trying to get rid of this tension."

"Okay. Good qualification. However, you are so intelligent and sensitive. I'm 99.9 percent certain that, with a touch of inward reflection, you can figure out why you chose these words and not others to describe your mom."

Athena ceases reflexively tapping her foot and lies down on her side. She begins tuning carefully into her breath, her eyes closing.

I suggest, "Creativity is consciousness in full form. There was a reason these particular words came up and out. Or, rather, that others didn't. Writing, like cooking, is as much about what you leave out as what you choose to include."

"I guess ... I mean, I *know* I was thinking about how afraid I am that things don't change. Or can't change. That being human is just reliving these repetitive patterns over and over until we die and are reborn to relive the patterns again. What if I'm fooling myself to think I can escape my mom's fate, and I'm only going to inevitably live her life?"

"I feel the fear and the antipathy in these words. The desire to differentiate yourself from your mom. But you are already your own person, Athena. How you untangle yourself from someone whose karma—whose very substance—is linked inextricably to your own is something different." I avert my eyes before she can argue. "I say this from experience. I spent many years demonizing my mother, making her wrong, inadequate. Finding and actively searching out the opposites in us. As you say in your last stanza, pushing on stone to remember the feeling of yielding."

"But it's insufferable watching her do things that go against what she says she wants. She wants to 'enjoy a meal together,' and then when we try, she talks obsessively about how many calories it contains and how what we're eating is bad. That is not enjoyable. She'll say she forgives my dad, then criticizes him for all the things he did wrong in their marriage. She says she is happy I am going to law school, then keeps mentioning how she wishes we could live closer or that I'd visit more. Oh, and she says ..." Athena rockets to her feet and begins pacing back and forth.

"What else?" I ask.

"She can't hold onto me. She couldn't hold onto my dad. She can't hold onto her youth. It's impossible. She can't hold onto ..." Fingers splayed, she shakes her open hands in front of her heart. "She's got to let go!"

"We all do. We are all asked to let go again and again and again. Surrender is an art unto itself. A continual practice—and very little is in our control."

"But I can't help her, Lila! I can't change her." She flings her arms out wildly to her side. Her hands slap her thighs as they land. "Ouch." She scrunches her face and shakes her head. "I cannot believe I just yelled at—I mean in front of—you."

"It's good. Something's happening. Honest emotion pouring forth points out where you're stuck."

"Jeez. Listen to me: 'I can't change her'? Trying to fix my own mom."

"No. No, you can't. You can't fix her or change her. But you can polish your own mirror. She may begin to appear a bit differently."

She cocks her head. "Is that like saying I should sweep my own side of the street?"

"It is. I like the reflection analogy because when I work diligently with what I see inside myself, it reveals and clears up many of the misperceptions I 'see' reflected outside myself."

Athena becomes still and closes her eyes a second time. She takes three concerted breaths. I mirror her breathing and feel her soften again. Recognizing her reflection, she gazes back at me tenderly.

"If a mirror's dirty, Lila, you can't see the image in it. And by trying to force myself to be so different from my mom, it is starting to feel like we're the same."

"When we apply the discipline required to change ourselves, the high unlikelihood of changing others becomes much more apparent."

A tendril of hair falls across Athena's eyes, casting a shadow down her cheeks.

I continue, judiciously. "I so badly wanted to change my mother too. Even in the womb, I felt how sad she was and that she believed I was the one who could remove her long-held sorrow. When she told me when I was ten that I was a healer, my heart vehemently responded, 'No, I'm not—I can't fix you!' I also knew I'd be required to face my own shadow before I'd be of help to anybody else. And how could I possibly do that as a ten-year-old?" I wink.

"Well, she was at least right about you being a healer. Why do you think I keep coming back here? Your voice, the way this entire place feels—I've never experienced anything like it."

I approach Athena and hold my hands out flat, palms upturned. She places hers on top of mine. We close our eyes and exchange the effulgent warmth from within as it reflects outwardly in the sun's rays blanketing the back of our necks.

"Can I have a hug, Lila?"

"Of course, dear."

We embrace amidst the verdant perfume of the lawn.

She lets go and steps back.

"Why didn't you want to be a healer? You're really good."

"I didn't want to be responsible for my mom, I suppose. Suppressing my gifts was a protective mechanism in case I failed—in case I couldn't heal her pain. When there's a desire, a true longing, to mitigate pain in this world, it can ache horrendously to touch into the heart of someone's suffering that might or might not be removed in this lifetime."

"What changed then? I mean, you said 'yes' to helping me when I reached out to you."

"I'm much older now, Athena. You asked for help with things I've experienced and worked with over the years— things I've really gotten into the grist of and come through more mature and alive!"

"Is that what you were doing while withdrawing to this place?"

"Yes, in large part. That, and creating an environmental offering—a sacred tribute—to this ephemeral world of ours."

I redirect my focus to the periphery. Slowly, I begin to turn in a circle, scanning and absorbing the heavenly green surroundings. Particles of light condense into prismatic colors and forms as trees and flowers, sculptures and stones. The interdependent arrangement between this outer body and my inner body came through patient years of effort and grace. The grace that lifts the veil of illusion, *māyā*. The grace removing any sense of being differentiated from what I am and what I see.

"Lila?"

"Yes?"

"What are you looking at right now? I mean, what are you seeing?"

"How exquisite this world is ... even the stuff we don't like seeing."

"Like my mom?"

"Oh, goodness, yes. Like your mom." I smile.

"I hope I can figure that out. When did it change for you?"

"When I realized it's most beneficial to focus on inner work—to 'polish my own mirror.' Over time, tensions eased up between my mom and me. Old stories and patterns tarnished. A freedom arose from beyond my habitual reactivity, and we could each exist just as we were."

"How did that work?"

"She changed when I changed."

"You're saying that when you did your inner work, she became different?"

"Or I did, allowing me to see her best attributes—attributes that had been obscured by my filters. As my teacher's fond of saying: 'My, how you've changed since I have!'"

Mātrikā's Muse

"That's like a ... what's it called? A koan."

"I'd like to ask you a question, Athena."

"Yes?" She looks up, eyes aflame.

"At what point do you tire of the contracted nature of the story you're living with your mom? At what point do you stop worrying about freeing her, which is not your job, and start investing in an effort to free yourself?"

She runs her palm across the long stalks of grass, as though gathering strength from their loose curls. "How can I do that?"

"In a thousand ways. Perhaps you begin with some deconstruction. Allow room for taking apart the story and then recreating your notion of this world you are so certain about." I lay the poem before her on the grass, angling the paper so that both of us can see the words. "Is this how you see it?" With my pinky, I underline "like a severed hand."

"Why not start here?"

"It's just a poem."

"You are a writer. You know as well as I do that words matter."

"Sure, but I told you that I wasn't really thinking about the words when I wrote them."

"No. You were in the creative flow, tapping into *Mātṛkā Śakti*, which is truly magical. But when it is used unconsciously or with mal-intent, her energy can cause great harm."

"What's that word you just used?"

"Matrika Shakti are the 'sound packets' that literally reverberate into matter, becoming worlds. *Matrika* originates from Sanskrit. It means 'Divine Mother' and represents supernatural sounds corresponding to the letters of the Sanskrit alphabet. These are the mothers whose sonorous, expressive powers give rise to the Universe itself."

"So, words create meaning, which creates lived experience?"

"It is something to consider. Our words shape our world."

"Is deconstructing a story or an experience, then, about

deconstructing your words?"

She seems disagreeable and tugs at a hangnail on her thumb when abruptly our attention is caught by the rat-a-tat-tat of a redheaded woodpecker a few pines away. Its furious drumroll continues as tiny flecks of wood dust fall like snow to the base of the tree. Then, as though it realizes it's being watched, the bird takes off in one wild beat of its wings. Athena sighs and looks down at her poem. She searches for an appropriate place to begin.

[Mātṅkā]

Dampness from the lawn weaves its way into my cotton pants, along my buttocks and thighs. Athena has come to rest on her back, holding the poem at arm's length and above her head as she studies it. Standing to adjust, I catch the sun reaching down through the weary paper. Light washes the words and projects them onto her face.

"Looking at the fourth verse, I suppose that this idea that she wants to hold onto the memory of her child's fingers when they were still small ... I don't think I was only feeling the mother's nostalgia. I also felt this enormous pressure as a kid to stay young, as though growing up and becoming who I'm meant to be was a betrayal. I resented my mom for making me feel that pressure. I ... I guess I still do. And I feel envious, so envious, hearing about other people's relationships with their parents that sound normal, balanced, healthy."

"I understand. Though by the time you're sitting in this midlife seat, you'll likely see that what other people say was perfect probably wasn't."

"True."

"We fabricate things sometimes when we don't know if it's

safe to share."

"But maybe it's also aspirational, Lila. Like you're suggesting: 'Write a new story to create a new world.'"

"And new experiences for ourselves."

"Do you think all of our ancestral stuff we're going through is related to karma?"

"Yes. And also, as women, we've been these incredibly strong creatures enduring so much for so long. Looking at my mom's life, she had heavy, heavy challenges, and the fact that she came through as decently as she did is miraculous. No, she wasn't as warm and attentive to me in the ways I wanted, but she gave me this life! I would not have this gift without her."

Athena whispers to herself, "No mother, no life." Sitting up suddenly, she pleads, "How did you forgive her enough to recognize that and not feel angry about everything she *didn't* give you?"

"By meditating—a lot. It is the promise fulfilled—that which can deliver you to the seat of your heart, the Heart of the Universe, the greater Self. Through meditation, I encounter a softness within my own heart, and it continues and continues to unfold."

"It is still unfolding?"

"It does. And this ever-expanding, surrendering heart field informs me on exactly how to work with challenges and continue to open doors to forgiveness. Today, I can say that maybe my view of my mom was not entirely accurate."

"Are you saying that what I say about my mom isn't real?"

"Not exactly."

"Then what?"

"Why do you resent her, or struggle to let go of your anger?"

"Because ..." Tearing at the grass, she searches for words. "Because I still want to be taken care of. No, that's not it. I want to *have been* taken care of. *Not be* the caretaker."

Blood rises in her face. Her breath diminishes again—choppy, sharp. I pause and retreat for a moment. Taking a long inhalation, I reach upward and outward to spread the air around with my hands, extending affectionate energy outward from my core through the twinkle of my fingertips. Athena's congested emotions disperse.

"What just happened? My whole chest relaxed." Blinking and squinting, she searches and exhales.

"There's nothing wrong with wanting to be cared for. That said, we must all learn to care for ourselves, Athena. If we don't, we aren't equipped to care for others. As I suspect was the case for your mom."

"I suppose so. It's impossible to give away something you don't have."

I run my hands lovingly across the poem a few more times, smoothing out the knotted energy of stored lineages. "Ultimately, meditation cultivates the ability to go inside and recognize your own already complete Self. Even in difficult times, you become capable of loving and comforting yourself. When you can touch inside and experience everything you need, you stop seeking to be taken care of by others."

"Lila?"

"Yes?"

"Do you think I use the entrenched story about my mom so I don't have to take on my own responsibility to grow?"

"That's a worthwhile inquiry."

Her repetitive yanking has uprooted a clump of grass, and she stares at it, suddenly sad, apologetic. She holds it up and tries to untangle the individual blades from the mass.

"I'd like to offer you something else," I say. She nods. "When my mom was dying, there was no one else she wanted around besides me. I knew that in this incarnation, it was part of my dharma to make her feel safe as she left. And I discovered I had the capability to do it. My husband said something to me at the time, which helped me finally drop the crossbow and arrow I'd been carrying for so long and deemed necessary for all the stuff my mom wasn't able to do."

"What did he say?"

"He reminded me that my mom never changed her last name to take that of her second husband's. He said, 'Your mom wanted so badly to remain identified with you, Lila, and your sister. You girls were the greatest creations of her life.'"

"Oh my. My mom never changed her last name either."

"My instinct," I say slowly, "is that there is a place somewhere in your mom's heart that feels the same way about you that my mom felt about me. She probably admires you greatly, even if she cannot say it or demonstrate it in the ways you long for. And you can either know that and continue to live your life in a regretful, remorseful way—or in a way that uplifts you and thus will come to uplift and benefit many others."

A breeze flips the paper over, and she reaches out to fix it, examining the words again.

"I'm curious about this verse here." I point lower on the page, where the ink is smudged from her writing so hastily. "About filling boxes with socks and tobacco and pillowcases."

"Hmm. I'm not sure. It's not as though those things were constantly scattered around my house growing up. Well, socks maybe. But I guess I was thinking about the sorts of things we hang onto when we aren't experiencing the love we feel we should have. How we think we can fill the gaps."

"Hoarding?"

"Yeah. Or even small collections." She picks up a gray pebble and runs her thumb over it, cleaning off the dirt. "I used to collect rocks and take care of them as though they were alive. You know, pet them and talk to them and ask them how they'd slept."

"You've always felt that sincere mother connection with nature, haven't you?"

She blushes.

"I've never thought of it in those terms exactly. But I think you're right. In the forest, I feel very … cradled. Why do you think that is?"

"There's a reason we call her 'Mother Nature.' Mother energy, Shakti, is what births everything into existence. Right now, you're hung up on a tiny fractalized experience of her creative force—this incarnation, your birth mother in this lifetime. Expand your vision, and you find the Divine Mother, the mother of this planet, the universes. She is also your mom, and the mother of your mom, and her mom, all creation. Her vital force is inside you and also out here, surrounded by all this." I wave to encompass the woods, the garden, and the sky. She follows the flow of my fingers as I touch the animating energy.

"Do you think we knew about this?" she says. "I mean, before we reincarnated, do you think we had a chance to see what we were going to experience in this life?"

"My teacher said it's not worth trying to figure out all the reasons why you exist in the form you inhabit today because the quantum physics of it is all too much. But I did have a feeling one time when I was meditating. I was standing in line at a kind of 'cosmic computer' and thinking, 'Am I ready to go back?' I was looking at the personal calculus: *You'll be a dancer, you'll be five foot eight inches tall, and you'll have a beautiful mom and dad, but things will break down and your sister will die. But you will help your mom heal.* I must have said yes to the entirety of it. I must have known I could be of some assistance to someone's well-being. To be of some use."

"So, nothing was 'being done' to you."

"No." I smile. "We are put into sets of circumstances to do what's right for those circumstances."

"Even with all the intertwined strings of karma, to have that control—wait—there's a better word: autonomy. To have that autonomy is a relieving thought."

"When I look back at this life, Athena, I can see how it's

possible that I manifested my own obstacles as a means for learning how to overcome them and to grow my capacity to love."

"You're making me think of what you said about the poison becoming the nectar. I had a therapist who had me pick out my favorite kid's book and read it to myself. I thought it was the nuttiest thing I'd ever heard of."

"And? Did you do it?"

"I picked out *Love You Forever*, which was actually my mom's favorite book, not mine, and as soon as I started reading, I began sobbing uncontrollably." Her fist closes around the pebble and squeezes. "It was like I was that little five-year-old again, wanting my mommy."

"You remembered how to yield. If you continue to seek the Self, what you really are, you will discover it. We are created to discover the creator. It's an easy mistake to blame our moms. To think they could do our work for us or give us the answer. Instead, they provided the key—they gave us our bodies, our embodiment."

"You aren't going to let me keep avoiding this, are you?"

"I love you. Why would I want you, or anyone for that matter, to avoid the place they must go in order to grow? To be truly happy. To discover bliss."

"I've been building this fortress around my heart for a long time, Lila. And then reinforcing it every time I speak about her."

"And wherever you've built up walls, that's where you take yourself out of life. Anywhere you say, 'I'm not going to go there, I'm not going to do this or that,' your heart reacts by continually closing down further and further. The more shut-down our hearts are, the more constricted we feel. It's interesting that you said you felt stupid; that's a concept, a product of the mind. In the Kashmir Shaivist teachings, the heart is said to be our entry point to discover our deepest wisdom."

"The heart, not the mind," she murmurs. "No wonder this poem was so constricting to write. I can't free my heart by living in my head."

"Can we try something I think might help?"

"Please."

"Try reading the first few lines of the poem. Then describe how they feel in your body."

"Okay." She drops the pebble beside her and tentatively reads the first stanza aloud. *"Count the minutes like calories— feel each one flay away your youth."* She pauses.

"What do you feel? And where do you feel it?"

"I feel anxiousness, here and here." She points to her abdomen and chest. "The need to grip hold of something. *Trace the deepening lines of each irrevocable wrinkle.* There's fear, like my legs are tensed to spring. *Save small hanks of your hair* ..." She looks away from the poem. "I don't even want to continue reading this, Lila. I feel more and more contracted; the words are triggering my nervous system into fight or flight. How does it ... do that?"

"*That's* the power of the Matrika Shakti, Athena! The power of sound. It is why mantra—sacred repeated words— is so effective; its sound reverberates within. Vibration has the potency to re-form us because we are, essentially, vibrating bodies of energy. Vibrational energy can be freeing or constraining. Each letter in the Sanskrit alphabet is considered a divine power in the form of sound. But harsh sounds and cruel words create bondage and ignorance. They can destroy wherever they're released to resonate."

"When the words are spoken out loud or written down? Or even when you think them?"

"Thoughts shape experience, too."

"So then, we're training our minds and creating our world with the words we use?"

"And shaping our subtle bodies. For example, a large part of my mom's disposition, her *vāsanā*, was one of dense grief.

She spent most of her time around people with traumatic lives and painful circumstances, subconsciously. I wanted her to contemplate that she was seeing mostly trauma because of her latent tendencies to speak and write about sorrow and suffering. By the time she passed, she hadn't exactly changed that, but I saw a certain wisdom arise as she left her body during death. Perhaps that repetitive behavioral pattern and its corollary samskaras were finally burnt off. My prayer for her was that her next adventure would be uplifting, lighter, and free."

"It's sad that she had to die to let them go."

"With yoga, we have the opportunity to process these familial traumas at any point." I notice Athena is slumping forward, her chest sunken in as though she's been punched.

"How do I prevent this? This anger that's coloring whatever I encounter? Can I clear it out?" she asks.

"Yes, it can—and will—neutralize, resolve. We could try another meditation if you like."

"Anything."

"Sit in a comfortable, cross-legged position."

She wriggles around, stretching out her hips. "Okay. I'm comfy."

"Do you feel okay closing your eyes?"

"Yes, I do."

"Gently close them, then. Take three long, slow inhalations and exhalations, releasing all the old air from your lungs. As you exhale, let go of anything you don't want. Now, begin to scan your body. Notice where you feel tight. Where do you feel receptive? Let the noticing be friendly and familiar. No agenda. Observe the breath, however it is."

We sit tranquil. A yellow swallowtail butterfly flutters between us, and bald eagles let out mating cries in the distance, just above the sparkling teal-blue water of Lake Washington.

"Now bring your awareness to your sitz bones and lightly

rock between them until you feel the triangle of your base plug into the earth. The front of your pubic bone is the upper point of this triangle, and the two sitz bones are the base. When you're settled, your spine elongates upward, naturally toward the sky. Your chin is slightly tucked."

With full commitment, Athena finds her asana. Her freckled face relaxes.

"Imagine the place two inches behind your breastbone, at the center of your chest: the hearth of your heart. Begin to send breath into this space, and observe it flowing in through the back of your body. Feel it expand the ribcage, the entire chest area. As the spaciousness increases, place a luminous altar in front of this hearth, creating a sacred mantle. It can be any color or material—golden or ivory or teak. If you can't see anything, just reside in the space, breathing and touching in through your back-body into the centering glow of your own heart."

Peacefulness completely envelops Athena for the first time. We could stay here a while or continue.

"On your next inhalation, imagine three rare cups made from precious gemstones. Maybe they are diamond or emerald, iridescent opal or amethyst. Place them with great care onto your altar. Take a moment to admire their beauty, their radiance—as the glow from within creates undulating reflections on the outside of each cup."

"Haaaa ... " she sighs out long. As her spine settles, it makes a popping sound in the thoracic area. She lets go a little further.

"Now, envision a quality you long for. Maybe it's health. Perhaps forgiveness, or love. When it arises, and you see the word clearly, drop the word into one of the cups on the shimmering heart altar. Feel how the word, how that quality, makes you feel inside your body—inside your cells."

Athena's spine suddenly jolts forward and returns straight. Another *kriyā*—an outward expression of inner purificatory energy—is moving, releasing. Her breath is almost invisible now.

"Ask for a second word—your heart's next desire. As you see it, place it in another cup. Drop it in. Let it absorb into your heart, into your body—you, your very essence."

Her head is folded all the way forward, stopped only by the weight of her chin sitting atop her clavicle bone. To an untrained eye, she looks uncomfortably awkward. I know she's close to a quiet state of dissolution and is likely no longer consciously aware of any verbal cues.

"Lastly, call forward a third quality. And allow your desire for this—and your desire for all three qualities—to become holy. To become a sacred yearning. To be real. You are everything you desire. Everything you desire, you already are."

We sit. Held, cradled, in samavesha. Everything hushed in a unified state of awareness, a quiescent place within this moment. And moment to moment, we remain until the sun begins its descent.

The evening air excites the surface of my skin as it composes itself into its cooling temperature. I come to. Quietly and lovingly, I whisper, "A-the-naa ... Aa-thee-naaa ... Aaa-thheee-naaaa." I hear her breath return, emerging from the still-point. "As you are ready, and it feels right, feel free to lie back on the lawn and rest, and connect yourself back into your body and our surroundings."

"Whoa."

"Take your time. No hurries. Just notice your normal breathing. Allow a few minutes to pass. Then, as you feel ready, slowly open your eyes."

I open my eyes and look down. Her face appears lit from within.

"Thank you," she whispers at last, and reaches her arms out wide and behind to unhook her bra, allowing her chest to expand even more. "That felt very healing."

"I'm so glad. Our deepest healing takes place by returning to that space again and again and again. The vast space within is where we meet our resplendent Self."

"But will I be able to get back there, to that same heart space? Can I do it on my own when you're not around?"

"Of course you can, dear. You can use this practice, your breath observation, your writing—any of those—as often as you need to reenter. One day, you won't need to envision anything to find that space in yourself. You will recognize that you *are* that space."

"Does the healing lie in what we *do* in our heart space, or is the actual healing taking place in our ability to finally enter a space of acceptance and love?"

"Healing is the permanently-seated awareness that we are composed of love."

"It's so strange. Underneath everything that I think is wrong, there's still love."

"Waiting for you to return to it. Love longs to express itself as us."

"Finally feeling it is so ... liberating."

"Love yourself and others in ways that liberate, Athena."

"Liberation, healing, love." She sounds the words out. Articulating them with her tongue, she tastes them. "I think each one makes room for the others to exist."

"Yes. They uphold one another."

She reaches for her paper, holds up the poem, and considers it. Then she carefully rips it into dozens of little squares and lets them fall to the ground, a miniature mountain of language. She scoops up the pile and lifts it into the air.

"I want these words to be free from one another," she

explains brightly, as the pieces of paper disperse on the wind, fluttering like moths. "I want them to form new sentences I've never even dreamed of."

rebirth: a love letter

mother
who teaches me how to whistle
and walk on plastic stilts,
how to read the newspaper and crack an egg,
how to hug grandma softly so her bones
don't creak,
how to build castles from sand,
pillows, cardboard boxes

mother who smells like peppermint
and cloves in her silky pajamas,
like firewood in her paint-rainbowed khakis,
who chainsaws branches off the oak
in our yard and for a week sweats
gasoline

mother with wrinkles like rivers
running down her cheeks—
when she smiles,
her mouth overflows:
an ocean

mother who spices our food in sharp,
confident pinches,
but rolls out dough
like brushing my hair
(languid, unhurried,
relieved right now
at how little life asks
of her)

mother who comes home from work
with tired voice and stone heart
so each day i have to chisel
her until the fractures
appear; she kisses my fingertips,
tells me that's why the swirled
prints grow there

mother who i once caught mid-cigar
on our porch, midnight,
smoke tangled like cobwebs
in her hair,
burning cherry orange
as a secret

mother who squeezes my hand, points—
    look, an eagle, there
    no—there!
and i don't see, but i gasp and squeal
anyway,
because she's crying
at something so
suddenly
alive

STORM

"Overhead, the clouds
twist around one another like
steely serpents."

[Mokṣha]

"Lila? Lila!" Athena's frantic voice bounces through the open garage, through the family room, and into the kitchen, bumping into me as I enjoy the last fragrant sips of my evening tea.

"Come in!" I call back, though she's already burst into the house. I hear her knock off her shoes as she sprints into the kitchen. I breathe out my solitude and welcome this new liveliness. "I thought you were leaving today?"

"Tomorrow morning, first thing. But I had to come by first. I'm just—all over the place." She is wild-eyed, flushed, vibrating with energy.

"Do you want to talk about your new adventure?"

"I know I'm interrupting, but—"

"If I felt you were interrupting, I would tell you." I rise from the table. "Let's go outside. Your energy seems a touch strong to be kept indoors right now, no?"

She nods gratefully and follows my lead into the terraced back patio surrounded with abundantly flowering planters, trimmed hedges, and the deep blue pond. The air hangs heavy and warm around us until an unusually chilly wind whisks by, snatching up fallen leaves and blossoms from the stones. Gray clouds are beginning to swirl and writhe overhead.

We follow a winding, pebble-strewn path to the orchard. Athena jumps up and hangs from an apple tree's ridged branches. Her ribs and intercostals stretched to their full length, she inhales and exhales fiercely. When she drops back to the ground, her energy settles a little, though her eyes still dazzle with electricity.

"Feel better?"

"Yes." She rubs her palms together, flakes of bark falling from between them. "It's impossible to watch my breath when I'm talking, so I've been trying to catch myself when I start to get anxious and notice the breath first."

"Very wise." I give her a rub on her high-held shoulders. "So, what's in that heart of yours?"

"Oh, Lila, it's been a … a tough day. While I was packing everything into my car for the move, I accidentally opened the door too quickly and the alarm went off. My neighbor's dog got excited and came charging across the street toward me. I don't know what made her do that—she's never left their yard before—but she came so fast, and this guy driving a pickup hit her. He didn't even have time to put on his brakes. It was so awful. I called 9-1-1 immediately, of course, and somehow managed to get a towel on the dog's neck, which was bleeding profusely. The dog's owners were absolutely beside themselves in total hysterics, so then I tried to calm them down too, enough that they could safely drive their poor hemorrhaging pet to the emergency vet hospital. It all happened in no more than maybe twenty minutes. But I've been so shaky and out of balance ever since. Lila, I could feel the dog's aorta pulsing through the towel. I still can. Like now it's inside my body too."

She presses the back of her hand to her mouth and shuts her eyes for a moment, locking me out. I touch her shoulders again.

"There's something more."

"I—I can't shake the idea that the dog was running toward me in reaction to hearing the car alarm go off. Like, if I hadn't been there, that dog wouldn't have gotten hurt. And maybe it was, I don't know, the dog's dharma or fate or something, but that doesn't exactly feel comforting, you know?"

"Seeing an animal hurt is never comforting, nor should it be. Let's untangle those two words, though: 'dharma' and 'fate.' Maybe you misunderstand what dharma truly means in a spiritual sense, rather than in a pop-culture sense."

"I thought it was the path of what's supposed to happen. Your destiny or whatever."

"That's why I don't like the ideas of fate and destiny. Those words are often used in a way that makes it seem as though you have no choice about your life's direction. Or that it's meaningless to cultivate discipline in how you respond to each task at hand. To me, fate feels like a dead-end street; dharma feels like answering a call. Whatever is going to happen in life will happen. Dharma is taking the next right step with whatever unfolds in front of you."

"Really?" She ponders the thought, slightly frowning.

"From my perspective, the way you describe this situation with the dog and the car, it was a dharmic moment for you. It unfolded in front of your eyes. We don't know why, and perhaps we don't need to know. But you did the right thing. You did the kind thing. And you didn't run away! You had your fearful thoughts *and* helped the dog while also supporting the frightened owners. You took the very best steps in the face of a distressing event. That's the right action without attachment to an outcome, just as the *Bhagavad Gita* teaches. In it, a young warrior, who is troubled about having to face war, speaks to God. The God figure encourages him to take the next steps and act to the best of his ability while letting go of any attachment to the results."

"Huh." She rubs her chest in a slow circle. "That helps. To think I acted the best I could."

"That's all we can ask of ourselves: Show up equally in all events, those we deem good and those we deem bad. We like to think we have control over outside circumstances, but we do not. Dharma is simply showing up to meet our duty with courage as life unfolds."

She shrugs, chewing on her upper lip.

"What else are you wrestling with?"

"It doesn't matter that much."

"Athena, come back to your body—notice where it is in this space." Her eyes take in the horizon. She takes a slow breath, and her teeth release hold of her lip. "It seems like you're holding yourself back from saying something. Do you feel that too, the biting?"

"Yeah, I did. Just then." She reddens. "It felt familiar—I must do that a lot."

"Perhaps more than you'd like to," I encourage lightly. "Now that you're practicing using your voice."

Her neck straightens. She steadies herself.

"I guess what I'm struggling with ... in seeing the dog get hit ... it made me start questioning everything. What if it was a sign that I shouldn't be going to law school? I've been feeling so positive these last few weeks, in touch with myself and my body in a way that I don't think I ever have. I feel like something is opening. Expanding. And now reality is setting in: I'm leaving tomorrow. By next week, I'll be in this new world surrounded by so many people with so many different energies. And as absolutely thrilled as I was—am—for the next chapter, I'm also really scared."

"Are you afraid a new environment will interrupt your yoga journey?"

"Yeah. It feels so easy to slip backward. You told me about

how you toughed it out for years working in politics, fighting against your dharma, and not recognizing it—to keep your job, to make money. How do I know that law school is actually my dharma, or if I'm dragging myself down the wrong path?"

"Do you feel like you're dragging yourself?"

"Not exactly, but how would I know?"

"There's nothing inherently dharmic or adharmic about you becoming a lawyer or about that end accomplishment. It is spiritually dissonant, however, to focus on the money and the title and then put the word 'dharma' on that. Money and success are karma. Dharma is the path of duty."

"You told me about how we all come into life with our karmic backpack. Facing and working with whatever's in mine is my duty, it seems."

"Yes. And over time, I've come to learn that humor and lightheartedness go a long way while we're doing that. Try not to stay too serious." I massage the ropy tendons running up the back of her neck.

"Oh, you mean I don't have to have it all figured out today?" She smiles shyly.

"Nope! Just show up and do your best!"

"The results will tell?"

"Sometimes. Sometimes we do excellent work and have congruent results, such as being accepted to a top-tier law school. Other times, our efforts are great, and the results are not. That we do not control. Using your abilities to do the best work you're capable of—that is the right dharmic action."

"I want to believe that so badly, Lila. But everyone's telling me this is about to be the hardest three years of my life. I'm not sure I'll be able to tell the difference between a dharmic challenge and an adharmic path."

"If you aren't able to pass your finals, that might be a clue. Or if you find yourself longing for another kind of work once you start practicing law—like if your spirit feels shut down. But right now, all you have to do is the next step. The work of the moment matters, *not* the fruit of it."

"Bite-sized efforts, accompanied by awareness," she summarizes.

"You'll discover if the challenge is sustainable or not. I tried to run a restaurant once—"

"You did what?" Her head lifts suddenly, and her jaw drops open as she whips around to question me.

"Yep, several years ago. My Jewish husband and I opened a deli. Our tagline was 'Tradition, updated' since we wanted it to be healthier than the Old World recipes. We served everything made from scratch with organic ingredients. Our graphic logo read *Naasay b'ahava* underneath.

"Made with love?"

"Yes! It was quite popular. Unfortunately, we couldn't break even. The labor to run a scratch kitchen is too costly now. And I wasn't willing to feed people processed food, something I would not do in my home."

"Honestly, that was a bold move, Lila. When you're cooking comfort food, everybody's own grandma does it better."

"True! That wasn't the real problem, though. The problem was that, for me, running a restaurant was altogether adharmic. The desire to nourish people, to cultivate community gathering, to do creative work—that was all very soul-satisfying. But the actual day-to-day stuff? I was not equipped. I'd never cooked in a commercial kitchen, only for loved ones. Who were we kidding, thinking we knew how to manage a bunch of cooks and servers who changed jobs every few months or frequently didn't show up to work? I was forcing myself into a role that left my nervous system shattered. I remember standing in the shower one day, my nerve endings raw as the water hit my skin. I thought, 'I will literally short-circuit if I keep doing this to myself.'"

"That does sound like a sign that's hard to miss."

"It was obvious. But you know yourself how easy it is to ignore your body's wisdom. The *Bhagavad Gita* also teaches that 'It's better to fail in one's own dharma than to succeed in the dharma of another.' Or, the way I think about it: I want to pursue the 'Yes.' The 'Yes' in myself, in my own heart."

A daring gust of wind rattles the tree branches as faint thunder rumbles from the northeast. Athena turns toward the growling sky, unconsciously squaring her shoulders and opening her chest to it.

"You ran away from home at fourteen," I venture. "Did that feel right to you?"

She nods. "I never would have done it if I hadn't believed there was a better way. My parents were constantly at each other's throats. They vacillated between being angry or sad or shut down. I knew life wasn't meant to be about creating tension and drama or hurting one another. I knew people could live contentedly, live peacefully. So, I went looking for them."

"How courageous. You heard your truth and followed it. See? You know the feeling of 'Yes.'"

"I guess I do. I mean, I knew it would be challenging whether I stayed home or ran away. And I did what I felt I had to do. Took my life into my own hands."

"That's admirable. Your genuine desire for your parents' happiness and peace led you to a righteous decision. When we want so badly for the people we love to be happy, it's easy to forget that we must tend to our own happiness. We forget to show ourselves the same consideration. We don't say, 'Hey, Me, I don't want you to experience such suffering. I want you to be happy—the same way I want all beings to have happiness.'"

"It's hard to say that to myself, Lila. It feels selfish."

"Though it's every bit as important. Otherwise, when

you go through challenges, you won't have any fuel for what you're facing."

"Maybe that's why I get so impatient."

"In times of crisis, I remind myself to 'put on my own oxygen mask first.' It's self-defeating to run around trying to help everyone else while ignoring your own anxiety or anger."

"Do you think the tools you've been sharing with me will transform these emotions?"

"Most definitely. I wish I had a time-lapse video to give you a peek back into my past! Yoga has revolutionized my life, Athena."

"Now that would be fun to watch. I do suppose I would rather be selfish than self-defeating."

"Do you believe it is selfish to attend to your own state? Or self-loving?"

Athena shoots me a grin. The thunder shouts again. It's within striking distance. Overhead, the clouds twist around one another like steely serpents.

"Do you really think I will be okay? That I can bring to school everything I've learned and practiced with you?"

"Of course you can."

"I wish I felt the kind of confidence you have."

"You will."

"Hearing you say that feels so encouraging."

"I went to school totally out of order—leaving high school at the age of fourteen. But I am intelligent and landed a full-ride scholarship to college at twenty-seven. And just as you are now, I was scared to death! I didn't think I was smart enough; my ego viciously repeated, 'You're never going to be able to do this.' But I spoke back to my fear and worked hard, graduating *summa cum laude*. Ninety-nine percent of our thoughts aren't true, Athena. I encourage you to challenge your thoughts, especially those that hold you back from your dream."

I turn and scan the horizon, permeated with a surreal amount of prospering, natural, living riches. I pause to recollect this sense of achievement, the sheer joy of accomplishing a momentous goal. Thunder claps!

"But early in, it didn't feel great," I continue. "I remember crying one day to my friend, Sister Kathleen, a nun from the order that ran my middle school. I wept as I told her, 'I feel awful trying to shove my heart up into my head.' I'd lived from the heart-space for my entire life as an artist, and in college everything became purely intellectual, so dry.'"

"Exactly, Lila—that's what I'm scared of too."

"Please try not worry. When we meditate and observe our breath and use our thoughts and words skillfully, we are bestowed with an ability to reside in our hearts *while* going about our ordinary daily lives in an extraordinary way. You will learn to reside in true nature more of the time."

"Even when undertaking a big challenge?"

"Yes. You don't have to leave any of your experience behind to succeed at school."

"What if I can't find this energy at school, though, Lila? I've come to be so ... so happy when I'm here with you."

"Oh, dear one! How could you ever lose it? Your happiness is not tied to this orchard or this garden or to me. It is inside of you. When we learn to go inside to the wise, radiant place of our heart-center, we start to recognize that the Divine is everywhere. She's not only in a temple or at home. You break down the mental barrier that falsely tells you that your meditation cushion is the only place where God is, but your law school class isn't. That's not true." I catch my reflection in teardrops taking form in Athena's eyes. "Wow—take a look at that!"

I point to the thick branch of an apple tree twenty feet from us. A red-tailed hawk rests, preening its speckled feathers, white chest stark against the darkness.

"Whoa. I've only ever seen hawks flying, never in repose."

"Even hawks have to rest sometimes," I suggest. The hawk turns its proud head toward us, and its black eyes flash. "You said it yourself, Athena: 'Kundalini is everywhere.'"

"Here, that's easy for me to believe. I see it in all this beauty. Really. It's just the other stuff, the struggles, the pain. Your sister and mom dying, my assault—my rape."

"It'll come. Have faith. When ovarian cancer rendered my mom bedridden, an urge to visit her daily percolated up seemingly out of nowhere. I kept thinking, 'This is nuts. How am I going to be in an oncology ward every day for ten hours?' But whenever I went there, miracles happened. When I looked closely at all those people in their beds with ravaged bodies, gowns in disarray, and only tiny patches of hair, if any at all, what I began to see were these glowing filaments of blue light inside their bodies. In all of them."

"Are you saying you were happy and that Kundalini was responsible?"

"I am saying that when Kundalini awakens, we become awash in oceanic love. We can see that surface appearances are not what things really are. The diseased bodies were made from the same aspect of light that I am. You too. And so, I lost my fear: I could be with my mom as she released her physical body, moment to moment. Each one was perfect and eternal."

"Did you process all of that suffering or did Kundalini do it?"

"If we tend to Her and take care, She will do the work through us. As She rises, purifying the body, She digests your trauma. It gets healed and released. Then we are no longer the doers of our lives."

The unsettled air around us catches stray, jagged debris on the ground. By some trick of up- and down-drafts, they're carried into a skyward spiral, rising higher and higher, dispersing wide and out of sight.

"Do you think," Athena asks, "that one person in a family can heal the entire family line? If I keep practicing, if I heal myself, could it help my ancestors or my descendants too?"

"Have no doubt. One committed spiritual practitioner can change everyone's trajectory. My teacher told me the healing I did with my mother at the end of her life will clear the samskaric patterns of our familial line for up to seven generations."

"Past or future, Lila?'

"In my case, past. I am the last of this familial line. There are no more of us."

"You mean …" she puts her fingers to her upper lip, knitting her brows.

"Yes. And when she said this, I made a commitment, a promise reaching back through my entire lineage—to my sister who died of an overdose, to my mom who could not fulfill her potential as an artist, to my yogi dad who never got to Ganeshpuri despite his long-term devotion to Guru Devi Maa, and to my grandfather. I said to all of them, 'I will carry all of you across the line because I am that strong. I will fulfill my promise.'"

"That's so selfless."

"Well, the magic of our individual unfolding is that it is interwoven with the collective's. When we begin to unpack this truth, we realize that all our autobiographies are mere chapters of a seismic, cosmological epic."

"So, it never really ends."

"Nope. Even when you shed your Athena Suit, you're still going to be around! But *this* body"—I lower my eyes and bow my head, forearms crossed in reverence over my chest—"these bodies we're inhabiting now, Athena—these are precious gifts. They are vehicles for our spiritual evolution. While I have one, I want to do the best I can on everybody's behalf."

"Don't you get tired, Lila? Of working on yourself while

also trying to help so many other people?"

"Are you asking if I'm tired of you?" I look directly at her, smiling.

She shrugs and looks away. I snatch a ripe apple off the tree and throw it to her. She catches it reflexively, startled back into connection.

"I rarely feel put upon. There was a time before all of this when I wanted to help everybody to the point of feeling imprisoned. But now? Now my desire to help is dharmic, innate. I want to wrap this planet in so much love that there's no choice, other than all living things being uplifted."

Athena grins. She takes a huge bite of the apple, and juice runs over her lips, covering her chin. As she wipes it off, a new thought sparks in her, and she speaks over the chunks of chewed fruit.

"Maybe this is a dumb question, but ... do you think the gurus get tired?"

"Hah!" I burst out, then catch myself when I see her face fall. "Sorry, I don't think that's a dumb question at all. I think it's a very caring one. And it's also impossible for me to know. What do you think?"

"I don't know if they get tired. But I think if I were a guru, I'd get frustrated."

"Why?"

"Well, they give all these practices and wisdom to their students, and people always want more, but they don't want to actually do the work. I'm thinking about when I took piano lessons in middle school. My teacher would get frustrated because I never practiced, and I'd still throw a fit in my lessons when I couldn't play the pieces. It seems like a natural human instinct—if you can feel power just by being around the guru without putting in any work, why would you ever choose to do the work when you're alone?"

"I suspect you're not far off. There are many people who

will tell the guru, or even beg, 'I need to be around you because it makes me feel so alive.' That's a hell of a way to throw away grace."

"How do we waste grace by begging a master to help us feel better?"

"We're playing weak. A master reveals a perfected path, *sādhanā*. We choose to develop our strength—to walk the path with faith and discipline, or lazily let it go."

"Is it adharmic to waste grace?"

"Once we have received grace, it is in our own hands. Do I want to be a lion or a sheep? And ..." I place my palms in prayer pose, laughing. "We all could use some help."

A massive jolt of thunder echoes above, and all at once the clouds open up, pouring rain down on us. Despite the sheltering crowns of the tangled apple trees, we are soaked within seconds, our clothes turning transparent and clinging to our skin. Athena drops the half-eaten apple and runs out from under the tree cover. Opening her mouth to the sky, she catches the pelting droplets on her outstretched tongue. Struck by her receptivity and pure joy, I run out too, stretching my arms wide to accept the downpour.

"I feel like dancing!" she yells out over the violent clash of the storm.

"So dance!" I shout back, leaping into the air.

She spins and spins and spins.

Another crack of thunder accompanied by blinding lightning slows her spinning. For a few seconds, it's too bright to see forms. Wind tears past us, ripping twigs and leaves off the trees, suspending them as they whirl in midair.

"Come on!" she calls and takes my hand, pulling me back toward the house.

Running through the driving rain, we stumble back up the path and through the wide-open doors. When we shut them behind us, the storm's fury softens enough that I can hear the water dripping off our hair and shoes. Athena is shivering.

"Are you cold?"

"A l-little." Her teeth chatter as she hugs herself.

"Let's change—you can borrow something of mine."

She follows me to my bedroom, and we strip off our clothes. I hang everything up to dry in the bathroom while she marvels at the red variegated stone walls.

"This is so cool ... like being inside the womb of the earth." She peruses the walk-in closet, humming to herself and opening unfamiliar doors one by one. "You have such cheerful clothes. All the colors." She pulls out a bright-red hooded sweater and rubs the loose-knit fabric against her cheek. "So soft—did you make this?"

"I did, actually. Do you want to wear it?"

"So much."

"Good. Here are the perfect leggings for it."

"This is so bizarre. It looks almost identical to this outfit from a dream I had a few nights ago."

"What was the dream?" I ask, piecing through a stack of brightly colored sweaters.

"Um. Well. Guru Devi Maa was there, actually. I've been having a lot of dreams about her since the start of this summer. Even though I'm not sure she's the right guru for me."

"My dad always told me, 'Watch out—that which you resist, persists.'"

"I hadn't really put a lot of stock in it. I thought I was dreaming about her just because of everything we talk about, but this dream was different."

"Were you wearing this in the dream?"

"No. *She* was! It was so vivid. She came to my house wearing this beautiful, red, hooded gown, surrounded by five swamis. Her forehead was marked with three white powdery lines and a crimson dot. She looked so intense, like she could rearrange the multiverse with her eyes. We sat around this big conference-style table in my living room and started to discuss yoga and philosophy."

I pause my clothing search to glance back at her.

"You talked yogic philosophy with Guru Devi Maa?"

"And five swamis." She nods slowly, as though entranced. "It was wild. I felt completely at home and also exhilarated. I was happier than I've ever been in my life. Like I was born for this. And then there was this moment where things sort of settled down, and she nodded once at the swamis and then slid a piece of paper across the table to me. It had a word on it—*Sari*. I didn't really know what it meant, only that it was significant. She sent the others away and then walked to the end of the table where I was seated. She knelt down in front of me, her enormous brown eyes welled with tears. And she said, 'Will you come live with me?'"

"And?"

"I woke up. I wasn't ready to answer." Athena takes the presented leggings and pulls them on. As she shakes out the hooded sweater, the bedroom light catches its streaks of interwoven gold. "Do you know what she meant by *Sari*? I thought that was just a dress-thing."

"Funny. That's only one meaning." I find a cobalt-blue wrap skirt and tie it around my waist, thinking. Hearing the rain tapping against the windowpane, I turn to listen and momentarily shut my eyes, conjuring images from Athena's dream. Words weaving within the silence.

"You might consider this: *Sāra* means 'essence' in Sanskrit, the heart of a teaching. *Sāri* could also be a feminine form of essence or a diminutive of *Sarita*, which means flowing. But you should search further. Sanskrit words have thousands of meanings if you look purposefully."

"It means 'princess' in Hebrew, I read. And that's so not me. Your ideas make more sense."

"Athena?"

"Yes?"

"She gave you a spiritual name. I do believe your dream was an initiation."

"You know what's weird? When Guru Devi Maa was asking me to come live with her, she was looking right at me—through me. She felt like a mirror, as though we were one. Like she was going inside of me and giving me my life back."

"Or reminding you of your greater Self."

"Yes. That's exactly how it felt."

"Remember this feeling, Athena, but without attaching any special importance to the unusual aspect of the experience."

Athena sits on my bed, playing with the duvet cover, tugging the knotted tassels on its corner.

"I feel so close to reaching a tipping point," she says, "a willingness to commit myself to all this. But there's something that's holding me back. I've been kind of anxious to bring it up."

I sit cross-legged on the floor in the center of the woolen rug.

"Yes?"

"I don't know. It might sound trivial."

"Does it feel trivial?"

"No. Not to me."

"That's all that matters. Go on."

"So many of these yoga teachings make sense to me—like I feel them in my bones. They resonate. Yet I keep getting hung up on Shiva and Shakti, this idea that Shiva is 'male' and Shakti is 'female.' Having them gendered feels too ... human, I guess. Constraining."

"Why have you felt anxious to mention this?"

"I mean, they're the two paramount principles in the teachings, so it feels sacrilegious to question them like that. But no matter how I try to visualize them, it doesn't sit right in my mind. Is that wrong?"

Storm

"I have no sense of 'this is right and that is wrong.' This is just a 'this.' In these teachings, Athena, it does not matter what sex organs you're born with: both energies exist inside and outside of you."

"I know. I feel them. So, the idea that we need to think of energy as male or female feels ... outdated. Exclusionary."

"Expressions of masculine and feminine qualities are not the same as gender. And whenever we seek to explain something in words, we limit it. Nonetheless, it is noble to try."

"Are there other ways to describe them?"

"Of course! Many."

"Such as?"

I consider the bedcover, which her nervous fingers continue to play with. "Shiva is the still-point. Space. The blue background on which the various forms take shape. Shiva is endless void, imperturbable calm. The single point of focus. And Shakti? Shakti is a Big Bang! Everything that springs from nothing. All of time. The infinite creative impulse, playing in the manifestation of innumerable forms."

"Like the garden, Lila."

"And your poems."

Athena slides off the bed and onto the rug beside me. We breathe in the subsiding cool air of the waxing moon.

"Do you absolutely promise I can take all of this with me when I leave? It feels so huge. I'm petrified of not doing things right, Lila."

"You have millions of chances to do things anew. Keep practicing. You are forming the only relationship that truly counts right now—your relationship with your innermost self."

"... The sun is warm in the snow and the rivers are running again ..."

"What is that?"

"From my favorite poem. And it's how I feel. Right now,

inside."

"Your enlivened words, your burgeoning wisdom, and your fierce commitment to justice will carry you forth, Athena. All your actions will flow reliably and strategically from this place. It's your karma."

"Wait—my karma?"

"*Karma* is action and outcome, while *jñāna* is knowledge or wisdom. Jnana is important, but it takes us only so far. Karma is significant, because if we don't act, we die. Your actions take on elevated forms once you know this."

"What's greater? Which one should I focus on?"

"The greatest is *bhakti*. Devotion to God, to Guru. Devotion to Self. Absolute devotion in all your activities. God is perceived when we experience God in every action of our lives. Can I tell you a secret?"

"Always."

Athena leans in. I feel her warm, cherished breath on my cheeks.

"It won't take you all the years it's taken me. I know it, I can feel it. You're heading off with an intention so ingrained. You are prepared—and you will discover *mokṣa*. Your own blazing light."

Suddenly, the room plunges into darkness. As the wind howls outside, I realize it must have blown down the power lines. Yet I feel oddly tranquil; my body informs me that there is no rush to find candles or flashlights. I am safe.

"Lila ..."

I can't see Athena, only the enfolding, velveteen throb of black.

"Yes?"

"I feel like we've done this before."

"I know we have."

The thunder rolls in again, a deep chant that vibrates through my veins. My blood is dancing!

"Maybe this time together it will be a little more ..." She

chuckles softly. "Graceful."

As I breathe into the darkness, I tell her, "I'm remembering something my mother said during one of the last times we sat together in the garden, listening to the birds: 'When you're quiet and attuned enough, the magic is written through you.'"

And I hear Athena's reply beside me, within me.

"Yes. Your entire life becomes the offering."

EPILOGUE
What Would I Give You?

I've often thought
    of what I would give
            you
  If *anything* could be
         given.

I still go back to a
      silent place
    Inside myself
       Where there is
         a knowing.

And I want that for
       you, too.
    That knowing place
       Where the
          Universe
            shines.

And when you enter
      there
you feel yourself as
  Privileged

Where you meet yourself
  and recognize
    The goodness
     of your spirit

Where you savor your
    uniqueness
  Celebrate your mind
  And care for all
    you are

I want you to know
 I met you there
  The day that
   you were born
With total wonder
 At the godliness
  Creation takes on.

I wondered at your
                    Perfection
    Praised the luck
       That loaned us
                  your days

Until you'd have grown
   And struck a
              bargain
   With the Universe

To explore all you could
   As you found yourself
     And measured
        against this
           world

Your specialness
    Whatever was yours
    Only yours to give

Looking at it all
   I understand
      What I've always
      Wanted most

For you to know
   How much is there
   Only yours to give

From your knowing
                 place
     Shall come your
         gifts
      To give this world
          some light

I'd give you self-love
   That you might
              love
      Strong wings
         To take
             Your flight.

Practices

Here are a handful of five-to-ten-minute real-life practices that have been pulled from this story. If you cannot be alone where you live, use a park, an empty classroom, or a public library's quiet room. Even the act of identifying places where you can be alone with yourself is important.

Some of these suggestions work with an activity. Some work with breath or minimal movement. Others work with the mind. Begin to discover which prompts make you feel safe, steady, and more relaxed. What makes you eager to learn more about yourself? What makes you happy? Where do you feel challenged? Working with a practice that feels good in the beginning both inspires us to do more and to employ that practice skillfully when experiencing the less free states that we encounter as human beings.

No matter what you like or dislike, most important is your effort to invest in knowing yourself. All wisdom, contentment, and meaningful success flow from the ability to rest in the state of self-awareness. Here we gain freedom. Here we are creative. Here we can guide ourselves through anything with our own power and knowledge. Have fun experimenting. Stay curious. Have faith in your ability to achieve your highest potential and shine!

[Garden]

Tend to Growth
Plant something. A seed outside, or inside if it's winter. Take care of the seed. Give it light and water. Observe the process. Or adopt a houseplant and repot it in a new vessel. Study its roots. Find where it likes to sit. Direct or indirect sun? Feed it. Determine how much it likes. Talk to it and wish it well. Notice how you feel about the process and the outcomes.

You can also try this with a virtue such as courage or kindness. Write the word in a place where you will see it and tend to it every day. Commit to its growth within and see how it takes root and sprouts in your life. Sometimes an external physical practice is easier to track than an internal one. Maybe try both and see which resonates for you.

To tend to growth, outside or inside, encourages openness and expansion. Tending grows *you*.

Sitting with Anger
Question what triggers anger. Write a list. Now watch for how many times a day it arises. Once there is an awareness of anger's comings and goings or its consistency as an emotional state, identify how anger feels inside your physical body. When you can name these feelings, look for an opening when you can step away from the perceived cause and spend time with anger alone.

Practices

When sitting with anger, keep your eyes closed or softly focused on a neutral object and observe the sensations in your body. Imagine ways to release them. If the anger feels fiery, let it burn through as high as the flames need to go. If it is dark and gray, let the smoke release into the wind and dissipate. If it is a color, let the color mutate. Allow all its associated images and sensations—or lack of them—be exactly what they are. Because anger spreads so rapidly, learning to work with this emotion is very skillful and yields results accordingly.

Sacred Offerings
Determine what you value the most. Find a symbol for it, such as a candle if you love light, a framed picture of your favorite person, or a religious icon. (There is no "right" one, only the one that speaks to your individual heart.) Keep this symbol in a place where you can sit and observe it, such as near where you sleep or on your person, if needed. Your treasured symbol could also be a tree or a body of water outside.

Each time you look at this symbol that you love, offer it something meaningful from deep within. A verbal prayer for a sick friend or a country at war. A flower infused with a personal wish. An offering of gratitude for your breath or heartbeat. If you're by a river, collect stones and infuse them with your offerings before throwing them into the water and observing their ripples traveling outward. Let creativity move this practice in ways that boost your desire to place sacred offerings into our world.

[Kitchen]

Eating for Energy

When it is mealtime, or you are hungry or tired, stop. Take three full inhalations and three long exhalations. Close your eyes and ask your body what it wants to eat. Then check in a second time: Will that food support how your body feels, not only in the moment but several hours from now, or tomorrow? Notice the response.

Eat the selected food quietly and calmly. When you're done, notice again. Try to name the energetic quality of the food as well as the energy of your feeling, now that you've eaten it. Pay attention during, right after, and several hours after eating. Do your food choices and eating habits sustain you throughout the day? Look for energetic cliffs, where your body tires post-eating, and for virtuous cycles, when your body feels better *after* eating than it felt *before* you ate.

Micromovements Before Mealtime

While doing kitchen prep or during meal breaks, occasionally do some stretches connected with your breath. Find a countertop, table, or chair. Place your palms down on the surface edge and walk your feet back while bending at the waist until your body forms an upside-down L shape. Stretch out your arms vertically overhead, allowing space for your shoulders to open, and place your feet hip-width apart, resting them flat on the floor. Soften and bend your knees if your hamstrings are tight. In this position, take 3 full inhalations and exhalations.

After your last exhalation, remain here, and on the next inhalation, arch your spine down (its midpoint toward the earth) and soften your belly toward the ground (cow shape). On your exhalation, arch your spine up (its midpoint toward the sky) while drawing your belly in (cat shape). Alternate your spinal extensions (cow) with flexions (cat), moving with your breath for three rounds.

Then stand up straight. Move your feet slightly closer together. Reach your arms up high overhead while keeping your shoulders relaxed and leaving space for your neck to remain long. Clasp your left wrist with your right hand and gently pull as you side-bend to your right, elongating the entire left side of your body. Then press your left foot into the ground as you straighten a bit, reach up long, and stretch again to the right. Think of the collarbones being wide and the heart space open.

Once you're in this position, inhale and exhale for three rounds. Rise up straight with your final exhalation and reverse sides with your arm clasp. Inhale and then side-bend to your left on the exhalation. Inhale and exhale for three rounds. Notice how your body feels.

Gratitude for Source
Digestion and nutrient absorption involve much more than the types of food we ingest. They're also affected by the state we're in before, during, and after eating. Encouraging the nervous system to relax prior to ingesting food can be simple, fun, and done anytime, anywhere.

Before eating, take one minute to sit with your eyes closed and to breathe slowly. Then open your eyes, and for another minute, take in your visual surroundings and what your food looks like. When you're settled, place your palms face down above your food to bless it and say, "Thank you to all of the energies that coalesced to provide this meal." As you eat, notice every enjoyable sensation (colors, flavors, sounds, and sights) and imagine yourself as healthy, strong, and fulfilled.

Cooking with Love
Prepare food for another, whether it is in the service of or out of love for a friend, neighbor, homeless person, child, or partner. Bring enthusiasm to it! Ask the person you are cooking for what they like or need, and if they have any special requests or dietary requirements. Connect your choices to their happiness and well-being. Imagine their delight in eating what you prepare for them.

Entertain the variety of color choices available and special touches you can add to lend joy to their experience. For example, if it's green broccoli soup, maybe shred some purple cabbage on top as garnish. If you are serving a meal, set a pretty table. If it's tea and cookies, place a flower or a small cut-out paper heart on the plate or in the delivery bag. As you make, arrange, and serve the food, send good thoughts from your heart through your hands, extending love into the offering.

[Studio]

Surrender to Self
Place yourself on the ground in child's pose (*bālāsana*). Curl up in a ball by sitting your buttocks on your heels, knees bent, and chest folded forward over your thighs. Let your forehead rest in front of you on the ground or on a soft surface, such as a rolled-up sweater or pillow. Place your arms alongside your legs and behind you.

If this pose is not accessible, lie on your side curled into fetal pose (*pārśva śavāsana*), or sit in a chair bent forward with your chest on your thighs or over a lap pillow while letting your arms hang loosely to the floor and your head hang forward. Let their weight drop. Once you've settled in this pose, imagine your breath expanding and filling your entire torso. Surrender into your body as you exhale. Remain here while breathing for several minutes, or 20 rounds of breath, or until your body feels some release.

Mātrikā's Muse

Nowhere to Go

Lie on the floor in any shape that feels good. Don't move until you are called from within to do so. Once you have been called, allow your inhalation to initiate the movement and an exhalation to settle it. Connect your breath to the movement. You might roll. You might stretch a tight limb, or move to one side or onto your tummy. You might sigh out loud, stretch all your limbs out long, or make any sound that wants to come out. There's nowhere to go, nothing to do. Move only to make another desired shape or a sound that brings comfort. Stay in this organic process for at least five minutes. When you get up, ask yourself, "Is it really necessary to get up *now*?"

Breathing for Release

Find a sturdy narrow cushion or stack a few smaller pillows. Sit on it in *vīrāsana*, or hero(ine)'s pose. Sit your buttocks on your heels with your knees bent and calves folded underneath your thighs and hips. Place the cushion or pillows between your legs, by the calves and under your bottom, to support and elevate your hips slightly above your legs.

Once you're comfortable and stable, allow your buttocks to relax and release into the cushion. Slightly shift side to side and settle in the center of your sitz bones. Take root and receive earth support. Soften your gaze or close your eyes. Imagine your spine naturally elongating upward from your base. Your neck is long and erect, chin slightly tucked, and your ears are aligned over your shoulders. Your skull balances on top of your spine. Sense your breath. Place your palms face up, with your right hand resting on the left hand on your upper thighs. Touch the tips of both thumbs together to form an open circle—the *Dhyāna mudrā* pose.

Observe your natural breath for a moment. Once you are settled, begin to breathe in a 1:2 ratio—meaning take a full inhalation while counting, then exhale slowly for twice as long. It might be 2 counts in, 4 counts out. Or 5 counts in, 10 counts out. The length doesn't matter; just allow the exhalation to be double the length of the inhalation. Notice the pause between the inhalation and the exhalation.

When you settle, begin to allow the inhalations and exhalations to occur as they naturally do. As you sit and observe your breath, imagine your torso as a cylinder. Play with the entire column, expanding it evenly all the way around as you inhale, and then gently contracting it all the way around as you exhale. Release.

Self-loving Light
Lie down on your back. Bend your knees and place your feet hip-width apart. Let your knees rest together and support each other. Place one hand on your low belly and the other hand on your heart. Try reversing which hands are on your

heart and belly. Stay with the arrangement that feels most connected and comforting. Take 3 rounds of slow breath. Settle into your own embrace and continue observing your natural breath.

Imagine bright white light pulsing in the center of your heart, two inches behind your breastbone. Direct its flow down your arms and into the center of your palms. Let this light and warmth pour into your chest and internal organs. If you do not find this easy to imagine visually, feel for the skin sensation of your palm's connection to your torso. Imagine that this connectedness and contact are nourishing you. Pour all your energy into yourself. Shakti is a powerful healing force, and our attention controls where She flows!

[Creation]

Spreading Prana
Stand or sit with your feet hip-width apart and arms hanging at your sides. Connect the four corners of both feet—your inner and outer heels and the ball mounds of your big and pinky toes—into the earth. Lift and spread your toes to activate your arches. Relax your toes back down. Once you feel firmly rooted, inhale through your feet, drawing energy

Practices

up through your legs, pelvis, and heart. Exhale and let this energy release.

Staying rooted, inhale to draw energy up from the earth through your body and into your arms as you raise them from your sides. Have your arms meet each other overhead, palms touching above your crown. Exhale while lowering your arms and hands, but keep your palms together to trace the midline of your front body. Let your palms come to rest in front of your heart in prayer position—*añjali mudrā*. Inhale as you lift your arms back up, straight overhead, keeping your palms together. Exhale as you separate your hands, rotate your palms outward, and lower them to meet your thighs, releasing and dispersing back to the earth whatever does not feel good. Repeat the whole sequence twice more, letting these rounds spread wishes from your heart out into the world as you exhale and lower your arms. Imagine it as reality.

Rewriting Pain

Take a pen and paper. Call to mind a challenging dilemma or relationship. Write out everything that is wrong with it for three to five minutes. Notice how your body feels as you write and afterward. Now, write about the same thing as if it is working ideally. Notice how your body feels. Look at and reread the words—the *mātrikā*—on the page and see if you can sense their sounds inside your body. Then toggle back and forth between your unfavorable and favorable reports. Take note.

Meditation on Heart's Desire
Take a seat somewhere that is comfortable and stable. Bring awareness to your sitz bones. Lightly rock between them until you feel the triangle of your base plug into the earth—meaning that the front of your pubic bone forms the upper point of this triangle and the two sitz bones form the base. When you are settled, allow your spine to elongate upward and naturally toward the sky, your chin slightly tucked under. Notice your breath.

Imagine the place two inches behind your breastbone at the center of your chest: This is the hearth of your heart. Send breath into this space. Imagine it flowing in through the back of your body. Feel it expand your ribcage and your entire chest area. When this spaciousness increases, envision a luminous altar in your heart, a sacred mantel. It can be of any color or material—gold, ivory, wood, whatever. If you do not see anything, just continue sending breath into the back of your body and into the center of your own heart.

On your next inhalation, imagine three cups made from

precious gemstones: diamond, amethyst, or whatever you see. Place them on your altar. Admire their beauty, their color. Then envision a quality you deeply long for, such as love or health. When it arises, visualize the word and drop it into one of the cups on your heart altar. Feel how the word and its quality feel inside your body—and your cells.

Ask for a second word—another heart's desire. As you see it, drop it into another cup. Let it be absorbed into your heart, into your body, into your very essence.

Call forward a third quality. Allow your desire for this to be so real that it exists. Allow this longing for all three words and qualities to swell within you. Make them a sacred yearning. Recognize this: You actually are everything you desire. Everything you desire, you already are. Breathe into this state.

When you are ready and when it feels right, let everything go and rest. Either stay seated or in *śavāsana* pose, lying flat on your back with arms down long, relaxed, and slightly away from the sides of your body. Your legs are extended, with some space in between them, and loose and relaxed. Gently wiggle your fingers and toes, or move in any way that feels good to connect yourself back into your body and your surroundings.

[Storm]

Circulating Shakti
Commit to encountering Shakti's force in nature. Pick your moment amidst a rain or windstorm, or on a very hot day, or in the snow. Assess for safety first: Make sure the conditions are not too risky and that you are feeling healthy and not too vulnerable. Then free yourself to feel. Know that you want to dance with Her power, that you are Her.

When the time arises, take five minutes to immerse yourself fully in the extreme weather. Stand in a downpour. Run into the wind. Lie or walk barefoot in the snow. Sit in the heat. As you do so, let nature's power permeate and circulate through you. Let its energy charge you. Then return to a quieter, less charged place and observe how you feel. Working with nature's outer Shakti can be helpful when we also work with strong inner emotions. Try viewing them as related forces.

Sacred Circle Creation
Take a pen and draw a big circle in the middle of a large sheet of paper. Close your eyes and begin to reflect upon what you most value. Brainstorm five to ten values. Maybe you value the environment and social justice; maybe it's God/dess or your teacher. See if you can name your top priority of this lifetime.

Practices

Once you've completed this brainstorming, write the items in a column in the center of your circle, perhaps placing the value you hold most dearly at the top and proceeding downward from there.

In the space on either side of this central column list but still inside the circle, write three to five other things that you value—animals, music, things that enrich your well-being. If you can't think of this many in the moment, leave space and add them later as they become known.

Outside and above the circle, write "_____'s Sacred Circle," filling in the blank line with your name. Beneath the circle, write "Anything outside, by permission only." Keep this drawing handy for when you are feeling uncertain about a big decision. Review it periodically and consider what actions you can take to keep yourself and your efforts directed inside your Sacred Circle more often.

Resting into the Void
Lie on your back next to a wall, railing, or piece of furniture that you can place your legs up against the back of or bend them over the top of. Your body is bent at a 90-degree angle from the waist. Your feet should be elevated far above your abdomen and head, legs either straight up in the air or bent

over the edge of the table or chair. If you are feeling unstable, place both hands on your belly. If you are feeling safe, stretch your arms out laterally over your head on the floor, hands touching comfortably. Listen for your breath.

Once you're observing your breath, begin to feel the blood from your legs reverse its flow toward your torso and brain. Notice how this nontraditional direction feels. As you rest, begin to imagine falling out of your back-body and into the night sky, stars, and celestial orbit. Ask yourself to let go. If any feelings of panic arise, mentally place somebody you love and trust underneath you as a sort of reverse parachute. Continue to fall back into space as far as you can go while watching your breath. This is a way to let go of your day before sleeping or release the past for the present.

OPEN-EYE PRACTICE FOR EVERY DAY

Prayer Walking, Prayer Presence
Pretend as though wherever you walk, things get better. Whatever room you walk into, whatever landscapes you pass by, whatever people you encounter—all of them become better than they were—smoother, healthier, uplifted. See how

Practices

long you can maintain this practice throughout your day while observing your breath. When you are not walking, try it in a meeting or in a social setting. Imagine each thing you say and hear as benefiting or shifting something or someone into a better state of ease and understanding for both yourself and others.

INFLUENTIAL Books AND Resources

Awakening Shakti
Sally Kempton
sallykempton.com

Becoming Kuan Yin: The Evolution of Compassion
Stephen Levine
levinetalks.com

The Bhagavad Gita
Eknath Easwaran
bmcm.org

Invoking Lakshmi: The Goddess of Wealth in Song and Ceremony
Constantina Rhodes

Meditation for the Love of It: Enjoying Your Own Deepest Experience
Sally Kempton
sallykempton.com

The Mother
Sri Aurobindo
sriaurobindoashram.org

My Life with the Saints
James Martin, SJ
loyolapress.com

My Lord Loves a Pure Heart: The Yoga of Divine Virtues
Swami Chidvilāsānanda
siddhayoga.org

Nothing Exists That Is Not Śiva: Commentaries on the Śiva-sūtra, Vijñānabhairava, Gurugītā, and Other Sacred Texts
Swami Muktānanda
siddhayoga.org

The Sacred Power: A Seeker's Guide to Kundalini
Swami Kripananda
siddhayoga.org

Secret of the Siddhas
Swami Muktānanda
siddhayoga.org

Shiva Sutras: The Supreme Awakening
Swami Lakshmanjoo
lakshmanjooacademy.org

Śiva Sutras: The Yoga of Supreme Identity
Jaideva Singh
mlbd.in

Start Where You Are: A Guide to Compassionate Living
Pema Chödrön
pemachodronfoundation.org

Tantra Illuminated: The Philosophy, History, and Practice of a Timeless Tradition
Christopher D. Wallis
ipgbook.com

The Tārā Tantra: Tara's Fundamental Ritual Text (Tārā-mūla-kalpa)
Susan A. Landesman
wisdomexperience.org

The Yoga of Discipline
Swami Chidvilāsānanda
siddhayoga.org

Acknowledgments

My mother, paraphrasing Isaac Newton, was fond of reminding me that "we all stand on the shoulders of others." She was teaching me that no individual human being can accomplish things alone. We need one another to learn, to evolve, to survive, and thrive!

In completing *Mātrikā's Muse*, as throughout my life, I have relied heavily on spiritual masters, colleagues, and friends. The following people and guides helped shepherd this story from personal practice to form. It is with great love and enormous respect that I acknowledge them:

To all enlightened masters, advanced practitioners, dedicated teachers, scholars, and artists who are beacons, sharing the fruits of their labor, yogic experience, and detailed scriptural exegesis: I am indebted to you and recognize that any mistakes contained herein are undoubtedly my own.

To Shira Herald, the invaluable early contributor, who invented the structure to eliminate any sense of ownership in Grace's touch: Our introduction was a hallmark of the Goddess: innocent in its arrival and explosive in impact. May your poetic talents, as demonstrated in "unwanting," "How to Live Forever," and "rebirth: a love letter," be rewarded beyond your wildest dreams, dear one!

To all young people: You inherently deserve an opportunity to fulfill your inner power in a world where humanity shows up to foster, safeguard, and invest in your new, spectacular creative visions of what the world can become. You deserve nothing less. You are the precious future as it desires to arrive.

To my beloved spiritual sister, Elisabeth A. Benard, and the undeniable Vajrayoginī for reuniting us. Your "thunderbolt" insistence that I offer up this book is its impetus: May it be of service.

To my spirit-buddy Eden, stepdaughter and shining star:

You have made me a better person, always reminding me who I really am. You are an amazing "why."

To Stephanie Renee dos Santos, aka Green Snake: Your friendship, light, and heart full of so much love is a safe mooring place for others on this journey. Your invitation to contribute to *When She Wakes* yielded a first chapter, and then this! And to the entire *When She Wakes* cohort: You are the wind beneath so many women's wings.

To Rita Goldman Gelman, real-life female nomad and author: Our shared times had tremendous impact on me as a writer, cook, and woman. Thank you for that fateful day when listening to me over lunch, you demanded, "Write the darn book! And don't bore me."

To my husband Jeff: Your stable nature, incomparable patience, and generosity of spirit wove the steadfast backdrop on which this time-consuming project became possible. I love you.

To my editor, Ceci Miller, for your keen perception, authentic encouragement, and word wisdom: Thank you for tenderly convincing me that "the rainbow can no longer be hidden."

To Constantina Rhodes and Devī Bhaktānanda for your precise and caring input on Sanskrit rules and exceptions for this nontraditional book: Your dedication to the preservation of the ancient language and respect for Mātṛkā Śakti are exemplary. Jai MAA!

To Ben Blue, for our thoughtful dialogues on gender, identity, and politics and their relationship to consciousness: Your gardening talent and creative insight are wonder-full.

To Shannon McCafferty for your unusually artistic book design that stretched my imagination in service of the audience I most care about—young women: May this tactile beauty welcome them in the front door of discovering their power and grace.

To the detail professionals, Mi Ae Lipe on proofreading and raising astute questions in the process. And to Nicasio Press for the final book copyediting and business details most readers never see. You brought clarity to complete what at times felt like an insurmountable task: publishing a book.

To my mom, for giving birth to me and teaching me to appreciate the many things that go unnoticed in the world. And to my dad, Mr. Marty, for his courage in ushering the Guru's grace into our lives. And to my sister, the smartest, prettiest, funniest, and second-best protector a little sister could ever want—I miss you. The epilogue "What Would I Give You?" is a poem that my mother wrote for me and my sister when we were young women.

To the Society of Sacred Heart nuns and Jesuit Catholic priests who gifted me an outstanding education, fostering my natural inclination for spiritual contemplation: *Ad majórem Dei glóriam*—for the greater glory of God.

To Scott Schwenk for pressing me to examine the Guru Principle.

To all my stellar and conscientious Hatha Yoga teachers over the years: Jo Leffingwell, Vidal Bitton, Kira Sloane, Bridgette O'Connell Becker, Jivani Jen Futterman, Chris Bennett, Melina Meza, Denise Benitez, Elizabeth Rainey, Claudette Evans, Ellie Rose, Beth Award, and everyone at Seattle Yoga Arts.

To my meditation teacher, the incomparable Sally Kempton, for your literary prowess and generous heart-imploding love that is felt everywhere, in this world and beyond.

To the Gurus Bhagavān Nityānanda, Swami Muktānanda, and Gurumayi—the Siddha Yoga triumvirate of perfected peace, power, and protection.

To the Supreme Being, for this opportunity to grow and to love again: Although you are given many names, you are the One from whom all life is given and to whom all life returns.

No End

www.ingramcontent.com/pod-product-compliance
Lightning Source LLC
Chambersburg PA
CBHW062048290426
44109CB00027B/2765